The Complete Guide to 2016 Movies: Volume 1
January to June

DAVID CRAIG

Introduction

I wanted to open this book with a really awe-inspiring breakdown of just why I love the film industry, something that would reduce all but the stoniest of hearts to openly weeping all over the pages. Sadly, I don't think that's going to happen.

In truth, I'm not entirely sure why I'm so drawn to film. It could be a whole multitude of reasons. Perhaps the fact that the fantastical adventures of our on-screen heroes offer some wonderful escapism in a world that we're told is full of natural disasters, terrorists, financial chaos and all manner of other terrifying things. Alternatively it could just be that, as even the earliest humans did, I love a good story. While back in the stone age people told tales through crude drawings across crackling fires, we tell ours by paying some beautiful people millions of dollars to say some words and jump around a bit. Why do I feel like the cave people come across as more civilised in that sentence?

I hope that in time I'll have some epiphany that will lead me to writing something far more elegant than this bizarre introduction you see before you, but until such time arrives I shall continue to write said nonsense wherever people will allow me. But why would I choose to write here? Aren't the remains of a dead tree somewhat irrelevant in the Internet age? To me, they are definitely not. I love books; physical books that exist in the real world, that is. While I'm quite aware that e-readers are being hailed as the future of reading, personally I prefer real books if only due to the soothing feeling of having something that doesn't require a memory card, a screen or a battery in this increasingly digital world. There's something quite liberating about knowing that no matter how long I read a book for, I'll never have to recharge it. There's also the fact that I'm worryingly clumsy, and if I drop a book from a height there's little risk of it breaking and if it does I've wasted about ten pounds as opposed to upwards of one hundred. I've dreamed of writing a book for some time now, and a book about one of my greatest passions seemed like an obvious place to start. They do say write about what you know, after all.

Which brings us to the book you're holding in your hands: what the heck is it? Well, *The Complete Guide to 2016 Movies* was something I originally envisioned would be a book you pick up once a week to see what films are coming out and whether you should care about them. I have quite literally written something about every major studio release hitting theatres in the first half of 2016, and arranged it in chronological order in the hope that this book would be of some use to people who hate the thought of spending money on a film that sucks. I do feel I need to justify the splitting of this book into two volumes. It wasn't something I originally intended to do, and it's not something I've done in a cash-grab manner reminiscent of a young adult film franchise. Honestly, I did it because I was running out of time. When I came up with the idea of writing this book I underestimated how long it would take me and after a few panic attacks and a number of days where I typed at my computer until I was in physical pain, I decided the two-part idea initially suggested by my mum might be best for my health and sanity. On that note, let's begin looking forward to the six months ahead of us and a year with more huge releases than ever before.

January

25th December – 16th January
The Revenant

The ongoing joke surrounding Leonardo DiCaprio and his failure to win an Oscar has been around for some time now, but thanks to the ever-growing presence of social media it really kicked into high gear with his 2014 loss to Matthew McConaughey. In 2016 DiCaprio tries once again for recognition from the Academy by teaming up with Alejandro G. Iñárritu, the director who won three academy awards in 2015 for his work on *Birdman*. Together the pair are the driving force behind *The Revenant*, which tells the true story of American explorer Hugh Glass who after being mauled by a bear is robbed and left for dead by his companions. Against the odds, Glass fights for his survival and journeys 200 miles across harsh terrain seeking revenge on those who betrayed him. So we have a highly-respected actor who has worked tirelessly for an Oscar, a director who has proven himself as Oscar-bait with numerous nominations and wins to his name, and a film that tells the harrowing true story of an American legend – this is bound to get DiCaprio that long awaited Oscar gold, right?!

Well, perhaps not. While things were looking very promising for *The Revenant* for some time, an eye-opening report about the numerous behind-the-scenes troubles the film has faced was published in the Summer of 2015, and suggests that it may not be the masterpiece we all assumed it would be. Much of the trouble this film faces comes from Iñárritu's decision to film only in natural light, and only in real environments rather than inside a film studio; the idea behind this is to put the cast of the film in an environment just as harsh as the one faced by the real people they are portraying. In theory, this is a nice gimmick, and former Oscar successes have utilised similar novelties to gain traction in the past, with *Boyhood*'s 'filmed over twelve years' shtick and Iñárritu's own *Birdman* gaining most of its attention on the back of how it was edited to look like it was filmed in just one take. But, with this particular artistic decision, the prolific director may have bitten off more than he can chew.

Filming only in natural light puts a severe restraint on how much footage the production can take in a day. Not only do they have to stop as soon as the sun goes down, but also it's very difficult to get the lighting to match between different takes when not in the controlled environment of a film studio; if the sky changes just a little bit between takes, it could wind up being jarringly obvious in the final product. This would be a tough enough challenge with even the calmest of directors, but reports from the set suggest that Iñárritu has been particularly picky about the scenes, calling for rearrangements just before shooting is about to begin. Then there's the physical torment that comes with filming in the extreme environments necessary to tell this story; DiCaprio talks of how his hands were numb after every scene shot, while allegedly an actor who was dragged across the snow in the nude in one scene was in severe physical pain – although it's worth noting that Iñárritu has claimed that this wasn't the case, that the actor consented to doing the scene and that plastic sheeting was put down under the snow to minimise the cold. Still though, that sounds pretty grim and I give serious props to the extra who persevered and got through it in the end.

Another tricky thing about the weather is that it has a habit of changing, particularly with the seasons. Indeed while the film began shooting in Canada, the production soon had trouble keeping the snow on the ground from melting as the weather got warmer. This led to the entire production being moved to Argentina to wrap up the remaining scenes. These delays have led to the film running severely over schedule; filming began in September 2014, and was intended to have wrapped by March 2015. Needless to say this never happened and filming was finally completed five months later in August. With this bloated schedule, comes a bloated budget; The Revenant began production with a budget of $95 million, a budget which has since escalated to a minimum of $135 million – and this figure doesn't include the advertising campaign that will have to be rolled out when the film is finally released. Rumours of crew members being frequently fired and replaced, and producer Jim Skotchdopole being banned from the set by Iñárritu have also surfaced, however just how much truth is in these rumours is anyone's guess.

Still though, Iñárritu has promised that while filming may have been laborious, the finished product will be well worth the struggle that went into making it. Indeed, art does often come from adversity and *The Revenant*'s impressive trailer suggests that it could well end up rising from the ashes of its tormented production. *The Revenant* is being released in late December in some territories (including the United States), but for some international movie-goers the film won't be hitting theatres until January meaning it just about qualifies for a place in this book. Besides, January's reputation as a dumping ground for bad movies suggests that awards contenders such as *The Revenant* and *The Hateful Eight* will probably be the only things worth checking out in the wake of the New Year.

25th December – 28th January
The Hateful Eight

After *Django Unchained* became a smash-hit and Quentin Tarantino's most successful film to date, it wasn't a huge surprise that the director expressed interest in returning to a Western setting for his next project. However, considering the success he had behind him, *The Hateful Eight*'s journey to the big screen was not an easy one and indeed it nearly ended up not being made at all. The story of this movie's tumultuous production begins in January 2014, when the project was revealed to be called *The Hateful Eight* and was expected to go into production in the summer of that year. All seemed well, and fans of Tarantino were eagerly anticipating this second Western, in spite of the revelation that it would not be a sequel to *Django Unchained*. Then the unthinkable happened: the script was leaked. In this increasingly digital age, film studios are finding it difficult to keep secrets about their upcoming projects with casting announcements and plot details often being revealed sooner then producers would have liked. However, it is rare that a film as major as this one loses its entire script to the depths of the Internet, and you have to wonder just how this colossal blunder came about. Tarantino himself has been pondering this very same thought, and claims that the leak was caused by one of three actors who had access to the script: Tim Roth, Bruce Dern and Michael Madsen. Which of the three it was exactly hasn't and may never be revealed, but the important part is that the leak nearly led to the project being canned entirely.

Indeed, after the leak Tarantino cancelled the film and instead expressed interest in publishing the script as a book rather than adapting it, seemingly in protest of the leak which it's fair to say left him very unhappy. At the tail end of January Tarantino filed a copyright lawsuit against the website Gawker, who had been responsible for hosting the leaked script. For roughly five months *The Hateful Eight* was in a state of limbo; it was unclear whether the film would ever get back on track, and when a live reading of the script organised by Tarantino took place in April 2014 things seemed more uncertain for the film than ever before. Then just one month later Tarantino announced that the film was back in production, just as suddenly as he'd announced its cancellation five months prior. From then on, it seems to have been smooth sailing for the project – Tarantino even withdrew his lawsuit against Gawker – and if I didn't know better I'd say the whole thing was some grand publicity stunt. However, in the interest of not being a sceptic about absolutely everything, I'm willing to give the benefit of the doubt. The film's cast was announced to include Samuel L. Jackson, Kurt Russell, Jennifer Jason Leigh and Channing Tatum alongside Roth, Dern and Madsen who had apparently been forgiven for allegedly being the cause of the leak. The script being adapted here is a later draft than the one presented at the live read, and reportedly this version has a totally different ending meaning all those who read the leaked script are now just as in the dark about this movie as those who never found the time. The officially released synopsis reveals that the film is about four strangers travelling to the town of Red Rock where a fugitive they have captive will be hanged. When a blizzard causes the group to stop at a stagecoach stopover, they then encounter another four strangers and quickly become embroiled in a deadly plot of betrayal and deception. The first trailer for the film was released in August 2015 to a warm reaction, indeed there's no denying that this has Tarantino's trademark style stamped all over it. Given that Tarantino is arguably yet to direct a bad film, it seems unlikely that *The Hateful Eight* will disappoint fans when it sees release at the beginning of the year.

8th January
The Forest

The first month of the year often brings with it at least one low budget, low quality horror film and in 2016 it looks like we'll be getting one right away in the form of *The Forest*. *Game of Thrones* star Natalie Dormer takes the lead as a woman looking for her sister in Aokigahara, a forest in Japan where people go to end their lives. In her search for her sister she is confronted by angry and tormented souls of the dead who prey on whoever crosses their path. The film is written by David S. Goyer whose previous horror credits include the critically panned *The Unborn*, which really doesn't fill me with confidence that this movie will impress. This film's release date right at the beginning of January, plus its inconsistent screenwriter suggests to me that this will be one to avoid, but hey maybe this film will end up surprising us; stranger things have happened, after all.

15th January
13 Hours: The Secret Soldiers of Benghazi

The second weekend of January will see controversial director Michael Bay take a break from his much-maligned *Transformers* franchise to direct *13 Hours: The Secret Soldiers of Benghazi*. The movie tells the true story of six members of a security team who defended the American diplomatic compound in Benghazi on September 11th 2012, when it was attacked by radical Islamic terrorists. It's questionable however if this movie will do any justice to the stories of these brave people; Bay is yet to direct a widely well-received feature with the director going as far as to say he "makes films for teenage boys," presumably his way of saying he makes mindless, explosive blockbusters – something that it should be said not all teenage boys are interested in. Whether Bay can handle the drama and emotion which presumably comes with a story such as this one then is currently in doubt, and the fact that the film is releasing in January – which as I've already mentioned is seen as a dumping ground for bad movies – certainly doesn't fill me with hope that this film could open up a more mature side to Bay's filmmaking.

15th January
The 5th Wave

Adaptations of young adult novels are a dime a dozen in Hollywood today, with very few of them actually proving to be critically or commercially successful. Still, studio executives persist in churning them out because the potential reward of finding the next *Harry Potter*-sized phenomenon is worth the risk of having a relatively small flop on your hands. Enter *The 5th Wave*, the latest of these adaptations which will also see release on the 15th January. The plot follows Cassie Sullivan, a young woman struggling to survive in a time where life on Earth has been devastated by an alien invasion. The film is notable for its strong cast which includes *Kick-Ass*'s Chloe Grace Moretz in the lead role, with *Ray Donavon*'s Liev Schreiber and star of cult films *The Guest* and *It Follows* Maika Monroe also on board. Still, it's questionable if this film will be able to forge an identity for itself, or whether it will just fade into the background with all the other failed young adult adaptations. On the off chance that the film is a hit, there are two more books in this series that could be adapted next.

15th January
Norm of the North

The 15th January will also see the first animated film of the year hitting theatres: *Norm of the North*. Coming from the small production company Splash Entertainment, this film follows the story of a Polar Bear called Norm and his three lemming friends who somehow wind up in New York City. Norm soon becomes the mascot of a corporation that plans to destroy his homeland. Let's cut to the chase here: this film is probably going to be terrible. The animation in the trailer looked unsettlingly bad in comparison to features from major production companies, while none of the jokes landed as they were presumably intended. Additionally, the lead role is being voiced by none other than Rob Schneider, an actor who has lost the respect of film critics and fans alike through his frequent collaborations with Adam Sandler. Parents looking to take their children to the cinema would be better off waiting another two weeks, as *Kung Fu Panda 3* on the 29th January will likely be a far superior film.

15th January
Ride Along 2

One of January 2014's most successful films – and also one of its most negatively received – was the Kevin Hart/Ice Cube comedy *Ride Along*. In 2016, the pair reunite for *Ride Along 2* which also sees director Tim Story and screenwriters Phil Hay and Matt Manfredi returning to fulfil their duties. The film is essentially an odd couple comedy pairing a veteran cop with one straight out of the academy: chaos ensues. If you were a fan of the first film then this one may also be to your liking, but those who disliked *Ride Along* need not apply.

22nd January
Dirty Grandpa

The 22nd January brings with it *Dirty Grandpa*, one of three R-rated comedies starring Zac Efron to be released in 2016. This one teams the *High School Musical* star with the legendary Robert DeNiro who plays Efron's mischievous grandfather. The film is essentially a road trip movie, following the hijinks that ensue as the pair journey to Florida together. DeNiro's comedic ability was left in doubt after 2010's critically panned *Little Fockers*, but there's a chance that Zac Efron's slightly elevated status after 2014's *Neighbours* could bring the best out of the veteran actor. The film also stars Aubrey Plaza from NBC's fantastic sitcom *Parks and Recreation*, and Adam Pally from a personal favourite of mine *The Mindy Project*. We can only hope that this strong cast isn't squandered, as with a largely unknown creative team behind the camera it's hard to predict just how this one will turn out.

22nd January

Risen

Religious films are becoming an increasingly hot commodity in Hollywood recently, with many including *God's Not Dead*, *Heaven is For Real* and 2015's *War Room* all doing solid business at the box office. The latest comes from director Kevin Reynolds (known for his work on *Robin Hood: Prince of Thieves* and the History Channel series *Hatfields and McCoys*), who helms this drama which chronicles the forty days following the resurrection of Jesus. The film stars *Shakespeare in Love*'s Joseph Fiennes, *Spooks* star Peter Firth alongside Draco Malfoy himself Tom Felton. The plot centres on a Roman centurion investigating the disappearance of Christ's body, while attempting to prevent an uprising in Jerusalem. Releasing alongside the raunchy comedy *Dirty Grandpa*, *Risen* may well end up doing solid business serving as counter-programming for those with a more conservative taste in cinema.

29th January
Fifty Shades of Black

Marlon Wayans has made a career for himself out of slapstick spoof films such as *Scary Movie*, *Dance Flick*, and *A Haunted House*; while the films are never warmly received by critics, they do usually succeed at the box office and it is for this reason that Wayans returns to the genre in 2016 with *Fifty Shades of Black*. The film is of course a parody of author E L James' erotic drama *Fifty Shades of Grey*, and stars Wayans in the lead role as Christian Black. Cinema-goers can expect much crude sexual humour and slapstick comedy, as is typical with these kinds of films. To be frank, *Fifty Shades of Black* is unlikely to be worth your time or money.

29th January
The Finest Hours

The final days of January will see another true story translated to the big screen in the form of *The Finest Hours* starring Chris Pine. The film is to tell the story of a rescue mission which took place in 1952, after a severe storm caused the destruction of two oil tankers off the coast of New England. Pine is to play Coast Guard Bernard Webber, the real leader of a crew of three who went out to save those aboard the tankers. The film is to be directed by Chris Gillespie, whose previous film *Million Dollar Arm* (another true story) was greeted with generally positive reviews but a lacklustre box office performance when it was released in May 2014. While

Gillespie seems to be a solid choice for director, screenwriter Scott Silver seems like a greater draw given his involvement in the critically acclaimed dramas *The Fighter* and *8 Mile*. The first trailer displayed some very decent CGI depicting the daring rescue; however I didn't find myself entirely convinced by the characters which seemed to lack some depth. Of course, you cannot possibly make a definitive judgement on a trailer alone, and *The Finest Hours* may still be worth your time; especially if you're looking to find out more about the United States Coast Guard and the difficult work they do each and every day.

29th January
Kung-Fu Panda 3

Dreamworks Animation has been struggling with its finances as of late, a sad fact which forced the studio to layoff five hundred employees back in January 2015 as it went on to make a fifty million dollar loss in the first quarter of the same year. It is then more important than ever that Dreamworks can turn a significant profit from their features, and in 2016 the first of two films they're hoping will get them out of the red is *Kung Fu Panda 3*. That isn't necessarily a bad bet either as the first two films in the franchise both made over $600 million, making this series one of the most profitable in Dreamworks' arsenal. This instalment sees Jack Black's Po reuniting with his biological father who takes him back to his birthplace, a secret panda paradise. Quickly though, things take a turn for the worse when an evil spirit named Kai begins stealing the powers of defeated kung fu masters, and using them to terrorize China. Po then takes it on himself to train the village of utterly harmless pandas into a band of kung fu pandas – hilarity presumably ensues. While I've never been a big fan of this franchise I have to commend the impressive voice cast that Dreamworks have assembled here. JK Simmons will be providing the voice of the aforementioned antagonist Kai, while Bryan Cranston will be taking on the role of Po's long-lost father. Meanwhile, series regulars Angelina Jolie, Seth Rogen and Dustin Hoffman are also returning along with Lucy Liu, David Cross and Jackie Chan. Whether this impressive cast equates to an impressive film remains to be seen, as ensembles such as this one have fallen short in the past. However the film is likely to at least please fans of the series as it comes from the same creative team as the previous two instalments, which have both been relatively well-liked by critics. Head of Dreamworks Animation Jeffrey Katzenberg has said that if the film is a success, he could see another three Kung Fu Panda films being made before the series comes to a close.

February

5th February
Pride and Prejudice and Zombies

The world has been gripped in an apparent morbid fascination with the zombie for quite a few years now, with the craze for shambling corpses seemingly kicked off with Zack Snyder's *Dawn of the Dead* remake in 2004. Since then, zombies have proven to be more infectious than ever before, with 2016 bringing with it one of the strangest zombie movies yet to hit screens. *Pride and Prejudice and Zombies* actually made its debut in 2009 in the form of a book written by Seth Grahame-Smith. The book combined the classic novel written by Jane Austen, with zombie horror elements added by Grahame-Smith and the result was a New York Times Bestseller. Yes, we live in a strange world.

Seth Grahame Smith's historical horror made its first foray into Hollywood moviemaking with 2012's *Abraham Lincoln: Vampire Hunter*. An adaptation of the book he wrote two years prior, *Vampire Hunter* received mixed reviews from critics and underperformed at the box office becoming only a very modest success. It is perhaps for this reason that *Pride and Prejudice and Zombies* has taken far longer to make the leap from page to screen. Still, it appears this feature may well end up being worth the wait, as it seems the folks in charge of *Pride and Prejudice and Zombies* have learnt from the mistakes made by Abe Lincoln.

For starters, one of the biggest problems critics had with *Vampire Hunter* was its overly serious tone, which many claimed didn't mesh well with the somewhat absurd premise of the film. *Pride and Prejudice* appears to be taking a more light-hearted approach; for starters, the film has enlisted the versatile writer-director David O. Russell to co-write the screenplay. While he has produced some duds, Russell has also proven himself very capable at tackling both comedy and drama, with films like *The Fighter* and *Silver Linings Playbook*. Also having a hand in the screenplay (as well as taking the director's chair) is Burr Steers. Steers has a less impressive filmography than that of Russell's, however his experience directing romantic comedies such as *How to Lose a Guy in 10 Days* and *17 Again* could prove useful in helping give *Pride and Prejudice* the comedic undertones it will probably need to attract mainstream audiences.

On the other side of the camera, Lily James has taken the lead role in the feature, portraying Elizabeth Bennett – the protagonist from the original Jane Austen novel. James seems to be a good fit for the role having conquered period dramas during her run on the critically-acclaimed *Downton Abbey*, while also making a splash in her first major leading role on film with 2015's live-action *Cinderella*. Joining her on-screen is former Time Lord Matt Smith, an actor who has struggled to find his place in the film industry since leaving *Doctor Who*. His role in *Terminator Genisys* last summer was intended to be the launch-pad towards bigger things for Smith, but after that film ended up being a critical and commercial disappointment, it's unclear whether Smith will be able to sustain a healthy film career in the long-term. The success, or indeed lack thereof, of *Pride and Prejudice and Zombies* could be the factor which determines the direction of Smith's career in the years to come. *Game of Thrones* stars Lena Headey and

Charles Dance will also feature in the film, with this strong cast leaving me optimistic that if nothing else this feature should deliver some entertaining performances.

Pride and Prejudice and Zombies will be released on the 5th February, a release date that would usually give it relatively little to contend with. However, this year sees the long-awaited debut of the *Deadpool* movie just one week after this film's release, and so *Pride and Prejudice* is going to need some good word of mouth to make sure it can maintain its audience in the weeks following the Merc with a Mouth's debut.

5th February
The Choice

February also brings with it the eleventh adaptation of a Nicholas Sparks romance novel – hooray! While these films certainly have an audience and generally turn a profit, they are almost universally disliked by critics and I would think that 2016's *The Choice* likely won't break that trend. Benjamin Walker (*Abraham Lincoln: Vampire Hunter*) takes the lead as a man living in a small coastal town who falls in love with a woman moving in next door. Other cast members include *True Detective*'s Alexandra Daddario, *Taken*'s Maggie Grace and *Smallville*'s Tom Welling. The film opens on the 5th February.

5th February
Dad's Army

Opening on the same day is *Dad's Army*, a feature film based on the classic BBC sitcom that aired from 1968 to 1977. The new cast includes many popular English actors including Toby Jones (*Captain America*), Bill Nighy (*Pirates of the Carribean*), Blake Harrison (*The Inbetweeners*), Michael Gambon (*Harry Potter*) and Alison Steadman (*Gavin and Stacey*). With such a strong cast I'm optimistic that *Dad's Army* could at least provide us with some memorable performances, although with the unproven director Oliver Parker at the helm it's hard to predict whether the film will be of any high level of quality. Still though, with an array of British talent and a name that still carries a lot of weight in the UK, the film should find an audience in Great Britain even if it struggles to find one overseas.

5th February
Hail, Caesar!

Another release dropping on the seemingly quite crowded 5th February release date is the latest offering from the Coen Brothers, *Hail, Caesar!* The directing duo have been responsible for a number of very memorable films over the years, with their recent directing effort *Inside Llewyn Davis* being particularly acclaimed. This latest offering looks very promising indeed, boasting a star-studded cast which counts Josh Brolin, Channing Tatum, George Clooney, Scarlett Johannson, Jonah Hill and Tilda Swinton among its numbers. The film tells the comedic story of Eddie Mannix, a 'fixer' working for Hollywood film studios in the 1950s whose job it is to keep scandals out of the press. While the project is said to have dramatic elements, it also seems to be a chance for the Coen Brothers to poke fun at their Hollywood peers. For example, the reason this film is called *Hail, Caesar!* is because while it follows Mannix's story, it will also be depicting the production of the fictional film *Hail Caesar: a Tale of Christ's Life* – seemingly a parody of the very real 1959 epic *Ben-Hur: A Tale of the Christ*, the remake of which is hitting cinemas just three weeks after this film. Additionally, Johannson is playing an actress who falls pregnant as her film is about to go into production – perhaps a reference to the situation Johannson actually found herself in during the filming of *Avengers: Age of Ultron*.

12th February
Deadpool

Created in 1991, Deadpool has quickly risen through the ranks of Marvel super-heroes to become one of the most popular characters in their universe. The so-called Merc with a Mouth has become so famous so quickly thanks to the humorous nature of his dialogue and his tendency to 'break the fourth wall' i.e. acknowledge the fact that he is a comic-book character. It remains then, utterly puzzling that in his debut film appearance all of the traits that have made the character so famous were essentially completely abandoned. Indeed, the initial response to the announcement that Deadpool would feature in *X-Men Origins: Wolverine* was one of pure, unadulterated excitement. A spin-off film for the character had been in development for the previous five years to no avail, but with the word from the set being that Ryan Reynolds was the perfect man for the role, fans were optimistic that *Origins* could be the launch-pad to that much-desired solo film. Then they saw the movie for themselves.

X-Men Origins: Wolverine is widely regarded as the worst instalment in Twentieth Century Fox's *X-Men* film series for a whole range of reasons, but one of the biggest for comic-book fans has to be its portrayal of Deadpool. That's right; the aforementioned Merc with a Mouth, perhaps the loudest character in the Marvel Universe spent much of his appearance in *Origins* with his mouth sewn up. I have no idea who approved of this decision but I don't think I'll ever understand their reasoning. They took away the major selling point of the character, and in the process alienated their most dedicated audience members: comic-book fans.

So what does all this have to do with the new Deadpool movie? Surely, Twentieth Century Fox have learned from their mistakes and abandoned this terrible incarnation of the character? Well, not exactly. Ryan Reynolds, who portrayed Deadpool in *Origins,* is back for this new movie but to be fair that isn't necessarily a bad thing. While fans universally disliked the Merc with a Mouth after his mouth-ectomy, they also agreed that Reynolds' did show a lot of potential in the role and seemed open to giving him a second chance.

As I write this the trailer for the new Deadpool film has finally been officially released to a very positive response, suggesting that the decision of comic-book fans to be reasonable and give Reynolds another shot could be about to pay off big time. At first glance, everything about this movie seems perfect; it's R-rated (something that Deadpool fans insist is the only way to faithfully make a Deadpool film), and Reynolds and the folks at Fox seem genuinely enthusiastic about delivering a movie that will please die-hard fans, something evident by how the costume Reynolds is wearing looks ripped directly out of the comic-books.

Needless to say that hype is through the roof, and it's because of this that I want to try and calm people down just a little bit. You see the thing with hype is that while it can be a great thing for a film to have, it can also end up taking a lot of the steam out of a movie's momentum. For a recent example just look at 2013's *Man of Steel*; would the film have been quite so divisive, would it have evoked so much rage among some comic-book fans if it hadn't been so unreasonably hyped up? But I digress. All I'm trying to say is that by raising this Deadpool movie to a place where it can't possibly be bad, we are inevitably setting it up to fail.

So what could go wrong with Deadpool 2016? Well, to start off the folks behind the camera on this film have a somewhat spotty track record, or in the case of director Tim Miller essentially no track record at all. Indeed, Miller is a relative newcomer to directing with his only other major directing gig being the three-minute prologue to arguably Marvel Studios most unremarkable film *Thor: The Dark World.* This is a little troubling as I've heard it on many occasions that being in charge of a big-budget production has something of a learning curve, so there's definitely risk involved there. Meanwhile, the writing duo behind the Deadpool script Paul Wernick and Rhett Reese, appear to be somewhat hit-and-miss. On the one hand, they were the writers behind 2011's fun comedy-horror *Zombieland,* but on the other hand they also penned the script to the much less fondly remembered *G.I. Joe: Retaliation.* This again, is potentially troublesome as Deadpool is a very hard character to write well. While many writers have crafted fantastic tales with the character, many more have tried and failed to harness the insane Deadpool-ness that makes the Merc with a Mouth quite so popular.

I'd hate for you to think that I'm rooting against Deadpool, because honestly I would love it if it knocked our collective socks off, and the first trailer has made me optimistic that it could. But, let's measure our expectations just a little bit with the intention of not giving this film something unachievable to live up to. Ultimately, the real battle this film is going to face is at the box office where recent R-rated comic-book movies have had a tough time drawing crowds. Sure, *Kingsman: The Secret Service* did remarkably well, but for every *Kingsman*-sized success there's a *Sin City 2: A Dame to Kill For* or *Dredd 3D*-sized flop. With this in mind, whether or not *Deadpool* does well financially when it opens February 12th could affect the future of R-rated comic-book movies for years to come.

12th February

Zoolander 2

Romantic comedy *How to be Single* also hits theatres on the 12th February, although will likely be overshadowed by the heavy hitters *Deadpool* and of course *Zoolander 2*. Ben Stiller hasn't had a lot of luck at the box office in recent years with *Night at the Museum 3*, *The Secret Life of Walter Mitty*, and *The Watch* all underperforming financially. By revisiting an earlier film there's no doubt that Stiller will be hoping to put some momentum back into his career, and there's a good chance he might do exactly that. *Zoolander 2* has a strong cast which includes Owen Wilson and Will Ferrell (returning from the first film), while Penelope Cruz and Kristen Wiig are joining the franchise in new roles. This cast should have comedy fans optimistic, while the promise of cameos from the likes of Justin Bieber, Kim Kardashian and Ariana Grande may also pique the interest of some people. Ben Stiller is also returning to the director's chair, which suggests that this sequel should be able to reproduce the same bizarre tone of the first. It remains to be seen whether the film will be appreciated immediately after its release, or whether it will take a few years to cultivate a fanbase as was the case with the first *Zoolander*.

19th February

Race

The next week will see the release of *Race*, the biopic of African-American athlete Jesse Owens who famously won a record-breaking four gold medals at the 1936 Olympic Games in Nazi-controlled Germany. Taking the role of Owens is relative unknown Stephan James, while the cast also includes Jason Sudeikis, Jeremy Irons and William Hurt. Director Stephen Hopkins has few notable credits to his name, and so it's unclear if this movie will give the story of Jesse Owens the justice it deserves. Additionally, the fact that the movie has a February release date seems to suggest that it isn't expected to be an awards contender; while some films released early in the year (e.g. *The Grand Budapest Hotel*) have received awards nominations in the past, generally serious contenders are released towards the end of the year. With this in mind, my expectations for *Race* are a little wobbly but it may well be a surprise hit when it's released on the 19th February.

19th February
Shut-In/Viral

The rest of this week's offerings all seem to fall within the horror-thriller genre starting with *Shut-In*, which stars Naomi Watts as an agoraphobic woman whose house is broken into. The film's most promising feature is its director Farren Blackburn, who was responsible for the acclaimed supernatural BBC TV series *The Fades*. Aside from Blackburn though there's little to suggest this won't be yet another forgettable home invasion movie, but only time will tell for sure. Low-budget epidemic horror *Viral* also seems unlikely to bring anything memorable to the table, but is likely to turn a profit coming from Blumhouse Productions – a company run by horror producer Jason Blum which seemingly hasn't had a major flop to date.

26th February

Ben-Hur

Of all the remakes and reboots to come out of Hollywood over the last few years, it is *Ben-Hur* that seems the most ambitious. A reimagining of the 1959 film starring Charlton Heston (itself a remake of 1925's *Ben-Hur*), William Wyler's biblical epic is seen as a true cinematic achievement by many, thanks in no small part to the huge scale of the production and the film's iconic chariot race sequence. Indeed, at the time of its release Wyler's film was the most expensive movie ever made with the production of over 100,000 costumes, the hiring of over 8,000 extras and the building of about 300 large sets going a long way to inflate the budget. Fortunately all this work paid off, with the film becoming a box office success in its own time (grossing about $150 million on a $15 million budget), while also staying in a position of high esteem to this day. In preparation for writing this book I finally sat down and watched the film – something I had to plan in advance due to it being just under four hours long – and I have to say it still very much holds up. Wyler's 300 practical sets have helped the film avoid the pitfalls of other releases from the fifties and sixties, namely those that depended more heavily on special effects and as a result now look incredibly dated. Of course the stirring performance by Charlton Heston in the titular role, as well as Stephen Boyd's turn as Messala – perhaps one of the most loathsome on-screen antagonists of all-time – also goes a long way in ensuring Ben-Hur ages as gracefully as possible.

With this in mind, it can be argued quite convincingly that *Ben-Hur* is a prime example of a film that doesn't need to be remade – the old saying, 'if it ain't broke, don't fix it,' comes to mind. Nevertheless a remake is what we're getting, and while I'm very doubtful that 2016's *Ben-Hur* could possibly stand up against the film released over half a century before it, it will at least be interesting to see how this story is changed to fit a modern audience. Remember, *Ben-Hur* is a **biblical** epic and indeed Jesus Christ plays a significant role in the film particularly towards the end. Therefore, it will be interesting to see if this 130 year-old story will be changed at all to better suit an audience seemingly more resistant to films with strong religious themes, than the audience of fifty or so years ago. Indeed, while many religious films have turned a profit in recent years this is helped by the fact that they generally have relatively small budgets – this is not the case for *Ben-Hur*. As a result, it seems unlikely that Catholic movie-goers alone will be able to carry this movie to financial success, and so the movie will have to appeal to a wider audience as well. One change that we're likely to see is in the film's depiction of Jesus; in the 1959 film Jesus' face was never shown, nor did we ever hear him speak as a result of the conservative attitude surrounding religion in those times. Now though, we're living in a world where a number of actors have taken on the role head-on from Max von Sydow to Christian Bale to Wilem Dafoe, and of course Jim Caviezel in Mel Gibson's controversial 2004 film *The Passion of the Christ*. Plus, given that the film has cast Rodrigo Santoro in the role – an actor with an active career which includes credits in the *300* series as well as the TV show *Lost* – it's a safe bet that Jesus will be getting some lines and perhaps even some more screen-time in this film than he has done in the previous two feature-length *Ben-Hur* movies.

But it's not just a modern audience that could cause changes to this classic story, but also the studio execs who are funding it who will likely want this remake to come to a more reasonable runtime than that of the 1959 film. As I've already mentioned the *Ben-Hur* film from the 50s was a little under four hours long, a runtime which those producing this remake simply wouldn't allow. Why? Well, the common theory for why we see so few mainstream Hollywood films surpassing the three hour mark is because the shorter the film, the more showings cinemas can offer, and the more showings cinemas offer, the more money film studios can potentially make. Of course, there are exceptions to this rule; Peter Jackson's epics *King Kong* and *The Lord of the Rings: The Return of the King* both ran over three hours, while Martin Scorsese's recent biopic *The Wolf of Wall Street* also hit 180 minutes. However, it's very rare for a major film these days to reach three hours, and so as a result a sizeable chunk of Judah Ben-Hur's story is going to have to be cut, which could make it all the more difficult for those putting this movie together to craft a compelling narrative.

It perhaps isn't all that comforting to see that the director of this remake is Timur Bekmambetov, a man whose recent directing credits consists of *Wanted* and *Abraham Lincoln: Vampire Hunter*. You have to wonder what made those in charge of this project think that a director who has only tackled action movies in recent years, would be a suitable pick for *Ben-Hur* - a story which does contain action, but perhaps not quite enough to warrant this creative choice. Unless of course, this is a hint that this interpretation of *Ben-Hur* will be more action-heavy than previous incarnations, a decision which in all fairness could prove an effective way of getting the blockbuster crowd interested in a film with strong religious themes. Surprisingly, the film has opted not to feature any 'big names' in the leading roles, that is, with the exception of Morgan Freeman who'll be playing Sheik Ilderim, the role previously played by Hugh Griffith in a performance he won an Academy Award for. Aside from Freeman however, the cast is decidedly lacking in star-power. Jack Huston – best known for his role on HBO's *Boardwalk Empire* – is taking the titular role, and he will be acting opposite Toby Kebbell as the villainous Messala. Kebbell impressed many of us with his stunning motion capture performance as Koba, the antagonist in 2014's *Dawn of the Planet of the Apes*;

sadly, the momentum he gained off that performance was stalled by his later involvement in the 2015 *Fantastic Four* reboot, where he again took the role of the villain but to a much less positive response. Rounding out the main cast is Iranian-born actress Nazanin Boniadi who will be portraying Esther, a character that Haya Harareet played so compellingly back in 1959. It could be said that the cast and director of this project leave something to be desired, however the saving grace of this remake could be in its screenplay which has been written by John Ridley.

Ridley recently achieved acclaim after writing the Oscar-winning *12 Years a Slave*, and his subsequent work on the critically adored TV series *American Crime* has solidified his status as one of Hollywood's most prolific writers. Indeed, his work on *12 Years a Slave* is a promising sign for *Ben-Hur*, a story which also approaches the subject of the immorality of slavery. Upon hearing that Ridley was chosen to write this movie, my expectations went from rock bottom to cautious optimism, however there's no denying that this film still has a lot to go up against even with Ridley on board. With a somewhat unknown cast (aside from Freeman of course), an unproven director helming the project, and the struggle of cramming Ben-Hur's expansive story into a reasonable runtime, if *Ben-Hur* is able to hold its own with the 1959 film it will be nothing short of a miracle. The film opens on the 26th February.

26th February

Kidnap

Halle Berry takes the lead role in Kidnap, a film about a mother who will stop at nothing to find her abducted child. The film has been in production since 2009, and is being directed by Luis Prieto whose previous work consists primarily of Spanish-language films. Berry found success with the slightly similar film *The Call* back in 2013, and seems to be crafting out a solid career for herself with these smaller projects while her involvement in blockbuster films appears to be winding down. In terms of quality, this film could go either way but fans of Halle Berry should be pleased to see the actress back on the big screen since her TV show *Extant* is struggling to hold viewers' attention.

March

4th March
London Has Fallen

Every now and then two films that seem remarkably similar just so happen to see release at roughly the same time, as was the case in 2013 with the release of *White House Down* and *Olympus Has Fallen*. Both films depicted Washington DC being put under attack by terrorists who take hold of the White House with the President inside. Of the two, more was expected from *White House Down* seeming as it came from director Roland Emmerich who launched his career by blowing up the White House in the 1996 sci-fi action film *Independence Day*. As it turns out, neither film received a particularly warm critical reception although at the box office at least there seemed to be a clear winner: the underdog, *Olympus Has Fallen*. Indeed, *Olympus Has Fallen* truly did look to be the lesser of the two films given its smaller budget, and less popular leading man (Gerard Butler to *White House Down*'s Channing Tatum). However, thanks in part to the aforementioned smaller budget and perhaps due to it being the first of the two films to see release, *Olympus Has Fallen* was the most profitable of the two and so three years later is returning for another instalment, something which I find myself strangely excited about. Don't get me wrong: *Olympus Has Fallen* was no masterpiece. The plot was somewhat silly and quite predictable, the CGI was at times surprisingly poor and you could say the film lacked some originality, drawing heavily from the likes of *Die Hard* particularly. That being said, I still found myself enjoying *Olympus Has Fallen*; I can forgive its unoriginality given that also in 2013 the *Die Hard* franchise produced its worst instalment to date, a film so bad it may well have killed the series. Additionally, a frequent guilty pleasure of mine is bizarre action films, it's the reason I find myself consistently returning to the ridiculous *Resident Evil* series, and perhaps also why *Olympus Has Fallen* struck a chord with me.

However, while I did enjoy the first film even I have my doubts about this sequel. For starters, the promotional material we've seen for the film so far seems to suggest it's a carbon copy of the first film in terms of plot i.e. the President is in peril, Gerard Butler must save him. Of course, it's hard to say definitively that this will be the case as at the time of writing we've seen relatively little from the film. However, from the officially released synopsis and teaser trailer it appears this movie isn't looking to break much new ground. Interestingly, the film was initially slated for release in January, something I found troubling as the first month of the year has established itself as a month dominated by two polar opposites: awards contenders, and films so bad the studio has given up on them. As *London Has Fallen* is certainly not the former, I had a bad feeling that it could well be the latter. Something which added fuel to this fire was the exit of director Antoine Fuqua who chose to move onto other projects rather than stick around for the sequel; he was replaced by Babak Najafi, a far less experienced director making his Hollywood feature debut with this project. However, back in September 2015 the film was rather abruptly moved forward to a March 4th release date, with one of the reasons given for this move being strong research screenings. If test audiences are giving *London Has Fallen* a big thumbs up then that could serve to alleviate many of the fears I had about this film, and indeed may be a sign that it will surpass our expectations when it finally does hit theatres.

Certainly Gerard Butler will be hoping *London Has Fallen* can surpass the original at least financially, as the actor's box office track record has been spotty since his breakout role in 2007's *300*. Indeed, *Olympus Has Fallen* was Butler's first major hit since Zack Snyder's fantasy adaptation, outside of the rom-com circuit that is where Butler briefly found success with *P.S. I Love You* and *The Ugly Truth*. If this sequel does find an audience though, Butler could potentially reinvent his career in the same way Liam Neeson did with the first *Taken* film which widened the actor's fanbase exponentially.

4th March

Grimsby

Sacha Baron Cohen became something of a hot commodity in Hollywood after his mockumentary Borat performed better than anyone ever expected it would, not only going on to make over $260 million on an $18 million budget but also earning Baron Cohen a Golden Globe award for Best Actor: Musical or Comedy. However after his subsequent projects *Brüno* and *The Dictator* saw diminishing critical and commercial returns, it seems slightly longer was needed for Baron Cohen's next starring vehicle to take shape. In 2016, he comes back to theatres with *Grimsby*, a film in which he plays an underachieving football hooligan whose brother is a slick black-ops spy (played by Mark Strong). Presumably the film will see the pair of them having to team up for a mission with hilarious consequences (at least in theory). Indeed, after *The Dictator* was a real disappointment my confidence in Sacha Baron Cohen's comedic ability was shaken, however there is hope that *Grimsby* could be a return to form for the actor. For starters, he's brought screenwriter Phil Johnston on-board whose previous work includes the much-beloved *Wreck-It Ralph*, whilst he's also broken away from director Larry Charles who helmed Cohen's last three pictures. In his place is Louis Leterrier, a director not known for working on comedies but who does have extensive history with the action genre, having directed *The Transporter*, *Clash of the Titans*, and 2008's *The Incredible Hulk* starring Ed Norton. This suggests that perhaps the black-ops side of Mark Strong's character could be played up, as the film attempts to deliver genuinely exciting action sequences alongside great comedy – something that 2015's *Spy* accomplished quite impressively. *Grimsby* has a strong cast which includes Isla Fisher, Rebel Wilson, and Gabourey Sidibe and so it certainly is well equipped to be the hit that Cohen needs to put the momentum back in his career. Opening on such a crowded week though, *Grimsby* will have to work hard not to be overshadowed by its competition.

4th March

Miss Peregrine's Home for Peculiar Children

As I've already mentioned, films based on young adult novels more often than not receive a cold reception from audiences, however rarely do they have the pedigree of *Miss Peregrine's Home for Peculiar Children* (henceforth I'll be calling it *Miss Peregrine* because the full title is just too darn long). *Miss Peregrine* is being directed by none other than Tim Burton, a director who seems to have become aware of audiences growing apathy for his collaborations with Johnny Depp. As such, his recent projects such as *Frankenweenie*, *Big Eyes*, and now *Miss Peregrine* have seen the prolific director branching out to some extent making them certainly more interesting than just another film where Johnny Depp acts silly in a wig. *Miss Peregrine* isn't a total departure from the dark themes that Burton made his name with though, as the novel of the same name follows a group of orphan children on a mysterious island where horrible creatures seek to destroy them. Burton is filming a screenplay written by Jane Goldman, a writer best known for her collaborations with Matthew Vaughn on the films *Kick-Ass*, *X-Men: First Class* and *Kingsman: The Secret Service*. I found all three to be very enjoyable films, and so I'm optimistic that the book by Ransom Riggs is in capable hands with Goldman, even if she's not working with Vaughn on this particular project. Taking the lead role is Asa Butterfield who has had a rough couple of years having been the face of box office flop *Ender's Game*, before narrowly losing out on being cast as the new *Spider-Man* in the Marvel Cinematic Universe. If *Miss Peregrine* is a success it could do some effective damage control for Butterfield, and perhaps even launch a new franchise for him given that a sequel to the first book was recently released. Joining Butterfield is Eva Green in the titular role, and Samuel L Jackson – a man whose career seems to be going from strength to strength with every year that goes by. While some would say that there's an exhausting number of young adult adaptations hitting theatres at the moment, this one at least has the potential to be very good indeed; let's hope that potential isn't squandered when the film sees release at the beginning of March.

4th March
Triple Nine

Another film seeing release on the crowded March 4th release date is the heist drama *Triple Nine*. The film has a star-studded cast which includes Woody Harrelson, Kate Winslet, Aaron Paul, Chiwetel Ejiofor and Casey Affleck, while two actors from opposing comic-book universes also join forces here with Anthony Mackie (Falcon) and Gal Gadot (Wonder Woman) rounding out the cast. The film follows a group of criminals and corrupt police officers who are being blackmailed by the Russian mafia, with the only way out of their unpleasant situation being to pull off a near-impossible heist. With an impressive ensemble cast on-screen and John Hillcoat, director of well-received dramas *The Proposition*, *The Road*, and *Lawless* behind the camera I'm very optimistic that *Triple Nine* could actually be a film worth our time. The talented cast and crew will also be working from a promising script by newbie screenwriter Matt Cook; indeed, the script for *Triple Nine* was featured on the 2010 Black List, an annual survey which finds the most well-liked screenplays in Hollywood that are yet to be made into films. Previous films from the Black List include the award-winning features *Slumdog Millionaire*, *American Hustle*, *The King's Speech*, and *Argo*. Of course, not every film picked from the selection is a gem but more often than not films from the Black List are of some level of quality, and it's for this reason that it has become so high-profile since it began in 2005. It's because of this that I'm cautiously optimistic that *Triple Nine* could be a surprise hit, when it's unleashed on audiences on the 4th March.

4th March
Zootopia

Zootopia – also known as *Zootropolis* in some regions – is the latest offering from Walt Disney Animation Studios, who have been on something of a hot streak as of late with the critical and commercial success stories *Tangled*, *Frozen* and *Big Hero 6*. These features have allowed the studio to navigate out of the shadow of fellow Disney studio Pixar, after a string of financial disappointments in the years 2000-2007 led to Disney's original animation house losing prominence in the genre it pioneered. Now at the top of their game, Walt Disney Animation is hoping to keep their new-found momentum going with this their first release of 2016. *Zootopia* is set in a world where the human race never came into existence, and so instead the world is ruled by anthropomorphic animals that live out their lives in much the same way as we do. They have jobs, they have mortgages and they have hopes for the future; for one rabbit (voiced by *Once Upon a Time*'s Ginnifer Goodwin) that hope has always been to work on the police force, but when she finally makes it she discovers being a rabbit on a force dominated by much larger, scarier animals is very difficult indeed. Determined to prove herself, she takes on a case that will require her to work with the sly scam-artist Nick Wilde (a fox voiced by Jason Bateman). The only other cast member currently confirmed is singer-songwriter Shakira who'll be playing Gazelle, the biggest pop star in Zootopia. Something of a strange casting considering Shakira's lack of acting experience, but as she's seemingly playing an animal version of herself perhaps this role won't require much acting talent. Choosing not to mess with a formula that has served them so well recently, Disney have brought in a crew that have helped make their recent projects so successful. The writer of *Wreck-It Ralph* Phil Johnston is penning the screenplay, while *Wreck-It Ralph* co-director Rich Moore will be joining forces with *Tangled* co-director Byron Howard to helm this project. *Zootopia* is shaping up to be solid family entertainment, but it seems unlikely that it will capture the hearts of audiences in the same way *Frozen* did three years prior.

11th March

Arms and the Dudes

Arms and the Dudes is a crime-comedy-drama film coming from the director of *The Hangover* series Todd Phillips, and based on a Rolling Stone article by Guy Lawson about two stoners from Miami Beach who ended up becoming unlikely arms dealers for the US Government. Filling the two stoner roles are Jonah Hill and Miles Teller; Hill is at a good point in his career at the moment, having gained Academy Award recognition for his role in Martin Scorsese's *The Wolf of Wall Street*, while also starring in the *Jump Street* movies which have proven to be strong box office performers. Teller on the other hand seems to be repeatedly rejected by mainstream audiences; the actor has found success in smaller features such as *The Spectacular Now* and *Whiplash*, but attempts to breakout in bigger productions like *That Awkward Moment* and 2015's *Fantastic Four* have not ended well at all. As a result it's difficult to predict how well this movie will do at the box office, especially when the talent behind the camera has such an inconsistent track record. The first *Hangover* film was a very enjoyable comedy however the two sequels ran the premise into the ground, and director Todd Phillips hasn't done anything of note since the franchise wrapped up. Meanwhile, the article this film is based on has been adapted for the screen by Jason Smilovic, a screenwriter whose only credits include the 2006 thriller *Lucky Number Slevin* and a handful of failed TV shows. Ultimately, I think *Arms and the Dudes* could go either way, but I'd certainly advise checking out some reviews before rushing out to see it when it hits screens on the 11th March.

11th March
The Free State of Jones

After ruining his reputation to some extent with a string of critically panned films including *Fool's Gold* and *Ghosts of Girlfriend's Past*, Matthew McConaughey pulled off an impressive revival of his career which really started in 2012 with the critically acclaimed independent film *Mud*. This was then followed up with a role in *The Wolf of Wall Street* and the lead in *Dallas Buyers Club*, a film that won him an Academy Award at about the same time the first season of *True Detective* was airing to much acclaim. In 2016, one of the projects McConaughey no doubt hopes will keep up this incredible momentum he's received is the drama-thriller *The Free State of Jones*. This movie is set during the American Civil War and tells the true story of Newton Knight, a deserter who leaves the Confederate army and retires to his home of Jones County where he marries a former slave. The film is written and directed by Gary Ross whose previous work includes the 2003 awards-contender *Seabiscuit* and the first *Hunger Games* film, and co-stars *The Americans*' Keri Russell and *Jupiter Ascending*'s Gugu Mbatha-Raw. This film is in a very strange position, being a relatively small production yet opening in a very crowded month, which sees most notably the release of Warner Bros. *Batman v Superman*. As a result, it could be difficult for this historical drama to attract attention; that is unless it stands a chance at being an awards contender itself. As already discussed, films vying for attention from awards ceremonies are typically released near the end of the year, meaning they're fresh in the minds of those in charge of deciding the nominations. While films released earlier in the year are sometimes recognised, it's less common and so it makes me wonder whether this film is of a high enough standard to run an awards campaign. If not, then it might be hard to convince mainstream audiences to buy into this movie when more anticipated releases are just around the corner.

11th March - 18th March

The Young Messiah/Miracles From Heaven

Earlier we touched on the rise of the religious film when we were talking about January's *Risen*, and indeed it's a narrative that will seemingly be popping up here and there throughout 2016. March brings us two religious films in quick succession, with *The Young Messiah* hitting screens on the 11th March, before just one week later *Miracles From Heaven* sees release on the 18th. *The Young Messiah* is a biblical drama based on a book by Anne Rice, which depicts a seven year-old Jesus who is just beginning to learn his identity and purpose. The film stars young Adam Greaves-Neal as the Son of God while Sean Bean plays Severus, a Roman soldier tasked with finding him. *Miracles From Heaven* takes place in 2011 and follows the true story of a 12-year-old girl who is suffering from a disorder which renders her unable to eat, leaving her forced to use feeding tubes for nutrition. After a near-death experience the girl not only makes a full recovery but also is cured of her disorder. The film stars newcomer Kylie Rogers as the young girl, with the star-power coming from Jennifer Garner who plays the girl's mother. The quality of religious films can fluctuate wildly, and the lack of any big names behind the camera makes it hard to work out if either of these films will be worth watching. Perhaps what will be more interesting is to see how they perform at the box office, as if *Miracles From Heaven* can withstand tough competition from the juggernaut *Batman v Superman* releasing just one week after, then it may well lead to yet more attention being brought to this genre.

18th March
The Divergent Series: Allegiant – Part One

Thus far, the films making up *The Divergent Series* seem to have been greeted with a collective shrug of indifference by mainstream movie-goers. The films seem just profitable enough to spawn sequels, without grossing anywhere near enough to stack up against their main rival *The Hunger Games*. The unremarkable nature of these films can also be applied to their critical reception, with neither of the two released so far impressing critics, but neither of them going so far as to offend them. In spite of this general lack of interest surrounding the property, Lionsgate is intent on adapting the final remaining book for the screen going so far as to break *Allegiant* into two films to get the most out of this rather modest cash cow as possible. And so, Shailene Woodley and Theo James return to this franchise for the beginning of the end, which will see their characters Tris and Four going beyond the wall enclosing Chicago to find a peaceful solution to the conflict within. Both the previous films in this series have had opening weekends of about $50 million, before finishing their runs with a worldwide total just under $300 million – you can expect a similar performance for the third time round. Although, and at the risk of sounding like a broken record, opening just one week before *Batman v Superman: Dawn of Justice* is going to be a tough challenge for this film to overcome. The reason I keep stressing this for the last few films we've talked about is only because the DC super-hero flick is expected to open very big indeed, and so smaller films such as this one might find their second and third week holds suffering as a result.

18th March

Monster Trucks

In recent years the animation genre has grown more and more competitive, having seen a sharp increase in the number of studios making animated movies. One of the youngest is Paramount Animation, a studio which burst onto the scene in 2015 with *Spongebob: Sponge Out of Water*, a film which brought in over $300 million on a $75 million budget. It was a strong start then for this studio in its infancy, but due to how strangely enduring the *Spongebob* brand is that wasn't hugely surprising. Their second feature *Monster Trucks* is less of a safe-bet. On the one hand the team assembled behind-the-camera seems remarkably strong; the film is being directed by Chris Wedge who helmed the first *Ice Age* film along with subsequent animated features *Robots* and *Epic*. The script has been put together by writing duo Jonathan Aibel and Glenn Berger of the *Kung-Fu Panda* movies, while the co-writer of the 2015 smash-hit *Jurassic World* Derek Connolly has also made a contribution. As a result, the cause for concern comes from less of a creative standpoint and more of a financial one. *Monster Trucks* has been in development since 2013, and has already been postponed twice (moving from May 2015 to December 2015, and then December to its current release date in March 2016). Perhaps as a result of this the budget has inflated to a sizeable $125 million, a figure that the film could find itself struggling to make back. Part of this is due to a lack of any starpower; while this is something some animated films can get away with on account of the fact that the actors don't appear on-screen anyway, *Monster Trucks* is a hybrid of animation and live-action. At the time of writing it's unclear which actors will be on-screen and which will be voicing animated characters, although *Suburgatory*'s Jane Levy and *X-Men*'s Lucas Till have been spotted running around on-set so presumably the pair of them make up a small segment of the live-action cast. While both are talented actors it's tough to say whether they'll be able to bring in audiences, and the remainder of the cast is also noticeably lacking in big names with perhaps the most recognisable cast members being Danny Glover and Rob Lowe.

Another problem this movie needs to overcome is the general lack of buzz surrounding it. Paramount Animation have been very secretive about this project, and as a result plot details are all but non-existent and the promotional material released for the movie so far equates to one poster. As I write this there are about five months until the release of this movie, and I'd wager that very few people outside of die-hard film fans even know it exists. As a result, I would really recommend that Paramount Animation release some form of trailer or synopsis, just to generate some interest around this property. A third factor which could affect the success of *Monster Trucks* is how popular *Zootopia* ends up being. On the off chance that the Disney feature takes off in the same way *Frozen* did then the family market could well be catered for by the time *Monster Trucks* hits screens. Then there's the big issue I've been driving home again and again for the last few entries in this book, and that's the imminent arrival of *Batman v Superman*. The week before its release all eyes will surely be on Zack Snyder's long-awaited epic, and in spite of its rather grim and mature tone the presence of capes may lead to some of *Monster Trucks*' potential audience members being led astray. Paramount Animation better hope this doesn't end up being the case, as although their first film was a solid hit that doesn't mean they can afford their second to be a colossal flop.

18th March
Midnight Special

Midnight Special is the fourth film from writer-director Jeff Nichols, whose previous projects include the critically acclaimed dramas *Shotgun Stories*, *Take Shelter* and *Mud*. With such a stellar track record so far, there are high expectations for *Midnight Special* which Nichols has described as a sci-fi chase movie. The film follows Roy (played by a staple of Nichols' films Michael Shannon), a father whose son has unique abilities. As a result of this he's being hunted by both an extreme religious sect and a government task force, leaving Shannon (along with allies played by Kirsten Dunst and Joel Edgerton) in a desperate race against time to get the boy to a safe and secret location. With Nichols at the helm and a very capable cast, I'm quite confident that *Midnight Special* will be an enjoyable feature – one that may even be able to withstand the colossal release of the following week...

25th March

Batman v Superman: Dawn of Justice

It could be argued that the DC Cinematic Universe stumbled out of the starting gate with 2013's *Man of Steel*. While the film was by no means terrible, it certainly didn't live up to people's gargantuan expectations; critics pointed to its lack of humour, over-reliance on action, and somewhat generic plot-points. Meanwhile, some comic-book fans were horrified to see what David S. Goyer and Zack Snyder had done to the character of Superman. No longer was he the face of optimism and the American way, rather he was the face of snapping necks and destroying cities in superhuman punching contests. Speaking as someone who was never overly excited to see *Man of Steel* – nor am I a particularly passionate Superman fan – I have to say I thought it was a solid film. Indeed, it is my belief (as I have already said in the Deadpool section of this book), that the reason for the hostile reaction to *Man of*

Steel was unreasonable hype generated by a copious amount of trailers and promotional videos.

It is then quite confusing to me that history seems to be repeating itself in the run-up to the release of *Batman v Superman*. Here we have the exact same creative team (Goyer and Snyder) tackling Superman once again, in a manner that seems very similar to *Man of Steel* (i.e. the much-coined phrase 'dark and gritty'). But rather than being cautious that the same problems *Man of Steel* faced could show up again in this sequel, many fans after watching the first two trailers are already declaring this to be one of the best films that will come out of the next year. As a result, *Batman v Superman* faces the exact same unreasonable hype that *Man of Steel* did just three years prior, and coming from the same creative team could well disappoint in a strikingly similar fashion.

To be fair to overexcited fans the world over, this is something that they've been patiently waiting many years for. Indeed, there have been rumblings of a Batman/Superman crossover film since the summer of 2001, with the film coming very close to being greenlit the following year. That obviously never happened which was upsetting to comic-book fans at the time, but in hindsight was probably for the best. The 2002 Batman v Superman script was written by Akiva Goldsman – a very hit and miss writer who at this point is mostly miss – who also wrote the forgettable *Batman Forever* and 1997's much-maligned *Batman and Robin*. After those two disappointing attempts at Batman, it was likely a blessing in disguise that Goldsman not get his hands on the character again. Indeed, the script to the doomed Batman/Superman project from over a decade ago was recently leaked online to a decidedly mixed response, and had the project moved forward and met its 2004 release date then Christopher Nolan's Batman trilogy would likely have never existed.

Since then it's been a difficult journey to where we are now, and it wasn't until the Marvel Cinematic Universe really started taking off that a Batman/Superman movie started to look like a real possibility. Of course, *Dawn of Justice* has since evolved to be much more than just a *Batman/Superman* crossover, and is now shaping up to be a miniature Justice League film with Gal Gadot's Wonder Woman confirmed to appear alongside rumoured cameos from other members of DC's premier super team. I hope just as much as the next comic-book fan that this film is phenomenal, but still I would advise caution as a film coming from a crew with such a spotty track record cannot possibly be considered a safe bet. *BvS* writer David S. Goyer may have had a hand in the Dark Knight trilogy, but that was with Christopher Nolan's supervision. With the DC Cinematic Universe now entirely Nolan-free it's unclear whether the writer of *Ghost Rider: Spirit of Vengeance*, *Jumper*, and the critically-panned horror flick *The Unborn* will be up to the task of putting together two of DC Comics' biggest characters. Meanwhile, many would say that Zack Snyder hasn't directed a good movie since his big break in 2007 with the box office smash *300*, while others would claim that Snyder is yet to make a good movie entirely.

Ultimately, *Batman v Superman* has a lot to contend with; it needs to establish a new Batman just four years after the most-acclaimed big screen interpretation of Bruce Wayne wrapped up, reconcile with those fans who were alienated by *Man of Steel*, introduce the first live-action Wonder Woman since Lynda Carter's fondly-remembered 1970s TV show, and prove itself a worthy competitor to Marvel Studios' rapidly expanding cinematic universe. Whether or not the film will accomplish these goals is really anyone's guess, but on March 25th we'll finally find out.

25th March
My Big Fat Greek Wedding 2

In the entries about movies releasing in the run-up to *Batman v Superman*, I've been warning of the risk that each film could get overshadowed by the much-anticipated super-hero feature. It is then quite a ballsy move that Universal Pictures have stood their ground and decided to keep *My Big Fat Greek Wedding 2* in the release date they assigned it in May 2015. Surely, this sequel to the 2002 Oscar-nominee is going to wither and die in the face of such strong competition? Not necessarily. While in the fourteen years following the film's release writer and star Nia Vardalos hasn't had the strongest of careers, it's worth remembering that the first *Greek Wedding* film is one of the highest-grossing romantic comedies of all time. Therefore, if this film gets as strong a critical reaction as the first one did, it could very well end up holding its own against the DC Comics goliath. Of course that's a big if and it is generally quite rare that comedy sequels stand up well against their predecessor, but with such a long break between movies there's a chance that the premise for this sequel will feel fresh and well thought-out rather than just being a retread of the first film – a pitfall some comedy sequels fall into. Additionally, one thing we've talked about a couple of times in this book is counter-programming i.e. two films targeting such wildly different demographics that they can co-exist without destroying each other. This is potentially another example of this: those excited to see *Batman v Superman* perhaps wouldn't be interested in seeing *My Big Fat Greek Wedding 2* and vice versa, so perhaps Vardalos' long-awaited sequel will be able to hold its own against one of the biggest films of the year after all.

April

1st April
Keeping Up With The Joneses

Keeping up with the Joneses is a phrase which refers to the idea that people don't want to look inferior to their neighbours, and so attempt to 'keep up' with what they're doing at all times. This idea is also the basis of a new comedy from director Greg Mottola and screenwriter Michael LeSieur, which follows an unfulfilled suburban couple whose lives are disrupted upon the arrival of attractive and charismatic new neighbours; the first couple grows suspicious and eventually discovers that their new neighbours are secret agents. The film's two leads are to be played by *Mad Men*'s Jon Hamm and *The Hangover*'s Zach Galifianakis, presumably the former will be playing secret agent opposite the latter's tightly strung suburban husband although that is yet to be confirmed. The film also stars *Now You See Me*'s Isla Fisher, *Workaholics*' Maribeth Monroe and the new Wonder Woman herself Gal Gadot. I'm really hoping that this film will come through as I feel it has a lot of potential; Mottola has proven himself as an effective comedy director having helmed *Superbad*, *Paul* as well as episodes of the fantastic US sitcom *Arrested Development*. Pairing him with a cast as strong as the one *Keeping Up with the Joneses* has recruited is a very promising move indeed, with the only worry now being the script by LeSieur whose only other major feature to date is the 2006 Owen Wilson comedy *You, Me and Dupree*, which received a lukewarm reception from critics and audiences alike. Still there's every chance that LeSieur could clear his name with *Keeping up With the Joneses*, and if he can then the product could be one of the most memorable comedies of the year. Indeed, if this film takes off it could also help launch Jon Hamm's film career as the critically adored actor has struggled to make the jump from TV, after box office disappointments *Friends With Kids* and *Million Dollar Arm*. The film opens on April 1st and as a result will see

Gal Gadot essentially competing against herself for box office victory, although it's quite a safe bet that *Batman v Superman* will retain the top spot.

8th April
Gods of Egypt

With a colossal budget of $140 million (not including advertising costs), *Gods of Egypt* is perhaps one of the biggest gambles of the 2016 summer movie season. The film is telling an original story i.e. not openly based on pre-existing material, following a conflict between the two Egyptian Gods Set and Horus as they battle for control of the Nile River Valley. Indeed, it's the lack of a pre-established fanbase which is causing concern from industry experts about this film's financial prospects, as the domination of sequels and adaptations has already led to *Gods of Egypt* having to move release dates from the 12th February to 8th April. In its original release date the film would have had to go up against both *Deadpool* and *Zoolander 2*, two films which would have inevitably gained more publicity and so perhaps would have overshadowed *Gods of Egypt*. The film's new release date of the 8th April holds considerably less intimidating competition; however the film still only has a week to really make an impact as the sure to be huge live-action *Jungle Book* film hits theatres on the 15th. This could also be a problem as the public's appetite for films involving ancient Gods has proven to be relatively small as of late, with 2012's *Wrath of the Titans* and even the young adult *Percy Jackson* films all disappointing at the box office. Additionally, while on the one hand the cast for this film is solid and includes *London Has Fallen*'s Gerard Butler, *Game of Thrones*' Nikolaj Coster-Waldau and Oscar-winner Geoffery Rush, the film has been criticised for casting white actors in Egyptian roles – a move also made by 2014 flop *Exodus: Gods and Kings*.

Indeed, it seems that in order for this film to succeed it may need to gain the critical acclaim that previous features based on Ancient Gods have failed to acquire. Director Alex Proyas whose previous work includes *The Crow* and *I, Robot* may be capable of accomplishing such a feat, but having the screenwriters of *Dracula Untold* penning the script is less promising. Ultimately, I think *Gods of Egypt* is one of Summer 2016's most unpredictable wild cards, and although I think there's a chance it could end up impressing audiences, there's an equal chance it could do quite the opposite.

8th April
The Boss

After a string of critically panned films which included *Identity Thief*, *The Hangover: Part III* and *Tammy*, Melissa McCarthy had damaged her reputation to some extent – a great shame considering the impressive breakout performance she gave in 2011's *Bridesmaids*. However, recently McCarthy appears to have been doing some damage control starring in the well-received *Spy* in 2015 and following up that new-found buzz in 2016 with the *Ghostbusters* reboot and *The Boss*; a film which sees McCarthy take the role of Michelle Darnell, a titan of industry who is sent to prison for insider trading and upon release finds it hard to win the forgiveness of all those she had mistreated. Starring alongside McCarthy are Kristen Bell, Peter Dinklage, Kathy Bates and Margo Martindale, a strong cast indeed but I can't escape the troubling fact that this film is being written and directed by Ben Falcone – who also fulfilled both duties for McCarthy's most strongly disliked film to date *Tammy*. Indeed, after that film was so unpopular with critics and audiences it's a wonder that McCarthy would agree to work with Falcone again – that is, until you find out that she's married to him. Yes, I can imagine it's quite difficult to tell your significant other that his movies aren't very good, but nonetheless if Falcone fails to deliver with *The Boss* then perhaps she should consider having that conversation as it's her career which is at stake.

8th April
Money Monster

Since 2011 Jodie Foster has expressed intent to do more work behind-the-camera rather than in front, helming Mel Gibson drama *The Beaver* before directing episodes of the high-profile Netflix series' *House of Cards* and *Orange is the New Black*. In 2016 she returns to cinemas, with her biggest directing gig to date *Money Monster*. The film stars George Clooney in the role of financial TV personality Lee Gates who gives out stock advice on his show which shares this film's title; however things take a dark turn after Gates is taken hostage by a viewer (played by Jack O'Connell) who lost all his money following one of Gates' tips. Clooney remains one of Hollywood's biggest stars, while O'Connell is a star on the rise having recently taken the lead role in Angelina Jolie's biopic of Louis Zamperini *Unbroken*. Pairing them together could result in some fantastic performances, and with an equally impressive supporting cast which includes Julia Roberts, Dominic West and Giancarlo Esposito there's real potential here for *Money Monster* to be Foster's most impressive directing job to date. The screenwriters attached to this project don't share the pedigree of the rest of the crew, but I'm choosing to have faith that this movie can live up to expectations given the quality of the actors on-board. Indeed, if the film gains a positive reception from critics, it may even be able to receive some awards nominations in spite of its release date which is spaced quite far from awards season.

15th April
The Jungle Book

The next two years are going to be an exciting time for fans of The Jungle Book, with not just one, but two live-action interpretations of the classic story seeing release. The first of which will hit theatres April 2016, and in my opinion is the more promising of the two. The film is coming from Disney, a studio that have proven themselves very capable of bringing their classic animated films into the realm of live-action, with 2014's *Maleficent* and 2015's *Cinderella* both being critical and commercial success stories. In the director's chair we have Jon Favreau whose previous directing gigs include the much-loved first *Iron Man* film, the less-liked but still solid *Iron Man 2*, and the classic Christmas film *Elf*. While Favreau had something of a wobble with 2011's *Cowboys & Aliens*, he appears to have recovered from that rather large flop and it remains the only critically panned film on his résumé. His 2014 indie flick *Chef* was seen as both a return to form for the director, while also serving as a low-budget palate cleanser before Favreau returned to the world of blockbuster entertainment with *The Jungle Book*.

The next impressive feature of this reimagining is the cast involved; while newcomer Neel Sethi will be playing the role of Mowgli, he'll be surrounded by a cast of highly experienced actors which includes Bill Murray (Baloo), Ben Kingsley (Bagheera), Idris Elba (Shere Khan), Scarlet Johansson (Kaa) and Christopher Walken (King Louie). The cast also features Lupita Nyong'o, who became one of Hollywood's biggest names after her stirring performance in the 2014 Oscar-winner *12 Years a Slave*. She's joined by *Breaking Bad*'s Giancarlo Esposito who rounds out this fantastic ensemble. But while things are looking good both behind and in front of the camera, this movie does have a wild card which could really go either way: the screenwriter. This film was written by Justin Marks – a relative unknown up until recently – with the only feature length movie to his name being *Street Fighter: The Legend of Chun-Li*. For those unaware, this movie – based on the popular series of *Street Fighter* videogames – is widely seen as one of the worst films of our time, and so it is both concerning and confusing that Disney would put him in charge of such a high-profile project. Still, as Marks has such a small filmography at the moment, it could be argued that he deserves a second chance, and that the ill-fated *Street Fighter* movie wasn't representative of his best ability. Indeed, things do seem to have heated up for the writer since getting *The Jungle Book* gig – having now been attached to both the comic-book adaptation *FBP: Federal Bureau of Physics* and the long-awaited *Top Gun 2* – suggesting Disney is happy with the work he did for them.

Still, hiring such an unproven writer for such a big-budget project is risky business, especially when just a year and a half after *The Jungle Book*'s release, another (entirely unrelated) live-action *Jungle Book* movie will hit theatres and will undoubtedly be compared to Disney's efforts for years to come. The **other** *Jungle Book* movie heading our way comes from rival studio Warner Bros., and goes by the name *Jungle Book: Origins*. The Warner Bros. feature has an equally impressive cast which currently features Christian Bale, Benedict Cumberbatch, Cate Blanchett and Andy Serkis (who will also be taking on directing duties). Indeed, where Marks is Disney's *Jungle Book* wild-card, Serkis may well end up filling the same role for Warner Bros. as the actor is making his directing debut with *Origins*. While he will likely face the challenges of every first-time director, the film's reportedly heavy use of motion capture performance could make the transition to behind the camera easier for Serkis than it has been for many actors before him. Serkis is after all widely seen as the king of motion capture technology, having donned the high-tech gear on numerous occasions to play entirely CGI roles such as Gollum in *The Lord of the Rings* and *Hobbit* films, and Caesar in the last two *Planet of the Apes* movies. It is foreseeable then, that using this expertise Serkis could bring out the best in the performers using motion capture technology for the first time.

Jon Favreau's *The Jungle Book* will see release on the 15th April 2016, while Andy Serkis' *Jungle Book: Origins* will come some time after on the 6th October 2017. Disney has something of an advantage in that they are first out of the gate, and the success or failure of their film could have a direct impact on WB's *Origins*. A high-quality product could increase the appetite of audiences for more *Jungle Book* adventures, meanwhile if the film disappoints then it could make audiences reluctant to see yet another live-action *Jungle Book* film so soon after they found themselves disappointed. Ultimately, only time will tell if these two versions of *The Jungle Book* can peacefully co-exist, or whether one must triumph over the other.

15th April
Barbershop 3

The *Barbershop* series began in 2002, and followed a day in the life of a struggling barbershop in Chicago run by Calvin Palmer (played by the rapper Ice Cube). The first two films received a generally positive reception from critics, although the second didn't perform as strongly at the box office – hence the twelve year gap between movies. Now though, Ice Cube is fast becoming a hot commodity in Hollywood having starred in the successful *Ride Along* films, taken a supporting role in the recent *Jump Street* movies while also producing 2015's box office smash-hit *Straight Outta Compton*. This increased status in Hollywood is quite probably what led to *Barbershop 3* finally being greenlit, and indeed it's quite possible the film could be the most successful in the series to date. The film is being directed by Malcolm D. Lee who helmed the well-liked *Best Man Holiday*, while a script has been written by Kenya Barris who has worked on the popular ABC sitcom *Black-ish*. *Barbershop 3* also stars Queen Latifah, Nicki Minaj and Cedric the Entertainer.

15th April
Criminal

Kevin Costner, Gary Oldman and Tommy Lee Jones reunite at last after 1991's *JFK* for *Criminal*, an action-thriller about an ex-con implanted with the memories of a dead CIA agent in the hopes that he'll be able to finish a crucial assignment. Ryan Reynolds and Gal Gadot will also appear the latter of which you may have noticed is having a remarkably busy year. Ultimately, I don't have a lot of confidence in this movie; it's being helmed by Ariel Vromen, a director with little to no notable credits to his name, while penning the script is the screenwriting duo behind *Double Jeopardy* and *The Rock* – neither of which are particularly well-liked films. Additionally, the film was initially set to be released in January which – as we've discussed multiple times – is never a good sign for a movie's quality. Therefore, I'd advise not getting your hopes up for *Criminal*, as while the cast may be solid it feels to me like this movie might have a little too much to overcome.

15th April
Everybody Wants Some

Everybody Wants Some is the latest film from Richard Linklater, a director whose career reached new heights in 2014 after his film *Boyhood* (which was filmed over twelve years) received recognition at the Academy Awards and the Golden Globes. He follows up what was perhaps his most acclaimed film to date with *Everybody Wants Some*, a so-called 'spiritual sequel' to his fan-favourite 1993 film *Dazed and Confused*. The movie is a comedy which takes place in the 1980s, and follows a group of friends during the last weekend of summer before college starts as they navigate their way through the freedoms and responsibilities of unsupervised adulthood. Personally, I really wasn't a huge fan of *Dazed and Confused*; I'm aware that I'm in the minority and that the film has built quite a following since its release, but the unconventional narrative just didn't engage me in the way it has evidently done other people. Therefore, I'm not quite sure how to feel about this movie. Ultimately, I'd be surprised if this film received anything other than a warm reception from critics – as almost every single one of Linklater's previous films have done – however, if you (like me) have struggled to connect with the director's work in the past it seems unlikely that you'll get much out of *Everybody Wants Some.* The film stars a group of relatively unknown young actors including Blake Jenner, Ryan Guzman, Zoey Deutch and Tyler Hoechlin and will see release on the 15th April.

22nd April

The Huntsman

I won't lie: I couldn't get to the end of 2012's *Snow White and the Huntsman.* I tried. I really tried. But the movie was just never able to grab my attention, quite possibly due to a bland performance from the lead Kristen Stewart. Stewart is an actress who has garnered much bad feeling from movie-goers thanks to her turn in the divisive *Twilight* franchise as Bella Swan. I actually don't dislike Kristen Stewart and I think she is capable of delivering good performances, unfortunately though her failure to do so in *Snow White* led to her being booted from her own potential franchise. Well, it may also have had something to do with her affair with the film's (married) director, Rupert Sanders. Indeed, after the film pulled in nearly $400 million at the worldwide box office, a sequel began to move forward which would have seen Stewart reprise her role. However, early in production the scandal hit celebrity gossip outlets the world over that Stewart had been having an affair with Sanders – who had been married since 2002 – while she herself was in a relationship with her *Twilight* co-star Robert Pattinson. The onslaught of bad PR this brought with it was the official reason for both Sanders and Stewart being removed from the planned follow-up, however Stewart's lacklustre performance surely wouldn't have made the studio executives eager to give her a second chance.

But Hollywood never gives up on a potentially bountiful cash-cow, and so began production on a prequel to *Snow White and the Huntsman* involving the two most successful elements of the first film; Chris Hemsworth's Huntsman and Charlize Theron's evil Queen Ravenna. Nick Frost and Sam Claflin have since also been confirmed to be reprising their roles from the first film, while *The Huntsman* has added some impressive new talent in the form of Jessica Chastain and Emily Blunt. Indeed, this film is shaping up to be something of a proving ground for every actress in consideration to play the Marvel comics super-heroine *Captain Marvel* in the 2018 film currently in development. Theron, Blunt, and Chastain have all been fan-favourites for the role at one point or another, and so seeing them in one film together could end up helping Marvel head honcho Kevin Feige in making his final decision.
Replacing Sanders behind the camera is Cedric Nicolas-Troyan who served as Visual Effects Supervisor on the first film, but is making his directorial debut with the second. While Troyan has never helmed a picture by himself before, he did act as Second Unit Director – aka the person who directs the less exciting scenes that the main director isn't interested in – on both the first *Snow White* film and 2014's *Maleficent* and so could well be

up to the task of taking on this high-profile project. No doubt *The Huntsman*'s two leads will be hoping it can thrive at the box office in spite of the first film's relatively lukewarm critical reception, as both Hemsworth and Theron could use a hit; Hemsworth has struggled to build a career for himself outside of the juggernaut Marvel Studios films, while Theron is also yet to prove herself as a box office draw with even last year's critically-adored *Mad Max: Fury Road* underperforming at the box office. *The Huntsman* hits theatres on the 22nd April.

22nd April

Keanu

No, this isn't a film about or even starring Keanu Reeves. In reality, *Keanu* is a comedy coming from Keegan Michael-Key and Jordan Peele – who made a name for themselves on their Comedy Central show simply titled *Key and Peele* – and follows a group of friends who have to go undercover in a crime organisation in order to save their cat who has been abducted. I'm assuming the cat is called Keanu because that is the only way the title of this film will make sense to me. The film stars the comedy duo in the lead role, and is written by Peele along with frequent collaborator Alex Rubens. The director Peter Atencio has also worked with the pair multiple times on their TV show, and so there's a good chance that Key and Peele's brand of humour should translate to the big screen quite well with this feature. The film also stars rapper-turned-actor Method Man, *The Last Man on*

Earth's Will Forte and *The Best Man Holiday*'s Nia Long among others. Given the success Key and Peele have found on the small screen I'm really hoping that they can put together a film worth watching with *Keanu*, however making the jump from television to film has been difficult to pull off for some and so we should be cautious about raising our expectations too high.

29th April
Eddie the Eagle

Eddie the Eagle is a film that tells the story of British skier Eddie 'The Eagle' Edwards, the man who through self-funding managed to qualify for the 1988 Winter Olympics and leave his day job as a plasterer behind. Well, supposedly it is anyway. Indeed, in the summer of 2015 Eddie himself (whose real first name is Michael) told the British media that he'd been warned by those producing the film, that about 90% of the movie is 'made up'. Hey, it isn't uncommon for films to take an artistic licence with the stories they're adapting, and this has made most audience members wise to the always suspicious tagline "based on true events". But in the case of *Eddie the Eagle* things seem particularly bad, and the Olympian has said he's anxious to see how the film depicts him. Taking on the role of Eddie is Taron Egerton, whose breakout performance in 2015's *Kingsman: The Secret Service* made him one of the biggest up and comers in Hollywood. The film also stars Hugh Jackman who'll be playing Eddie's coach Bronson Peary, a man who never existed – yes, the departures from Eddie's actual life become astoundingly clear upon closer inspection of this movie. Still though, just because it isn't faithful to the facts doesn't necessarily mean this movie won't be any good. It's coming from director Dexter Fletcher whose work on the British films *Wild Bill* and *Sunshine on Leith* has been generally well received, and has a strong cast which includes the aforementioned Egerton and Jackman, alongside Hollywood icon Christopher Walken. Indeed, while the film may not please Eddie's most loyal fans given its departure from the true makings of one of Britain's favourite underdogs, *Eddie the Eagle* could well end up being worth our time anyway.

29th April

Nine Lives

On the same weekend that Walken makes an appearance in the *Eddie the Eagle* biopic, so too does he appear in the bizarre comedy *Nine Lives*. This high-concept comedy tells the story of a workaholic businessman played by Kevin Spacey, who must figure out how to redeem himself after an accident leaves him in the body of a cat. Yes that's right folks, we've seen body swap films before with *Freaky Friday* and *The Change-Up*, but this may well be the first movie about a human being swapping bodies with a cat. Walken plays the owner of a mystical pet shop somehow connected to Spacey's predicament, while the cast also counts Jennifer Garner and *The Flash*'s Robbie Amell among its numbers. At first I thought this film sounded like an utter disaster for all involved, but I'm starting to wonder if *Nine Lives* might be so odd that it actually ends up surprising us by being a genuinely entertaining comedy feature. It is after all, coming from director Barry Sonnenfeld whose previous work on the quirky TV series *Pushing Daisies* as well as the *Men in Black* films, might give him just enough weirdness experience to make this premise into a good movie. Or it'll be bloody awful. One of the two.

29th April
Mother's Day

A trend that I blame *Love Actually* for is the creation of a genre of movies which follow large ensemble casts at a certain time of year. The pioneer of these films has no doubt been director Garry Marshall who became romantic comedy royalty after directing the much-beloved *Pretty Woman*, but in recent years has discredited himself with the much-despised seasonal films *New Year's Eve* and *Valentine's Day*. In 2016 he'll no doubt make more money from this weary premise, as *Mother's Day* hits theatres with rom-com staple Jennifer Aniston in the lead role. Aniston impressed many film fans in 2015 with her performance in the flawed drama *Cake*; indeed, the film itself was by no means excellent but her performance in it gained her a Golden Globe nomination, and so it's unfortunate to see her going back to her old although likely far more lucrative ways with *Mother's Day*. The film stars other big names in the rom-com circuit Kate Hudson and the pretty woman herself Julia Roberts, while Jason Sudeikis takes the male lead. If you enjoyed either *New Year's Eve* or *Valentine's Day* then there's a good chance this film will also be to your liking, everyone else need not apply.

Ratchet & Clank

Three weeks before the *Angry Birds* movie hits theatres in May, Sony's *Ratchet & Clank* makes its long-awaited big screen debut. The film is based on the popular series of Playstation videogames that have been running since 2002, and sees much of the voice cast of the games returning including James Arnold Taylor and David Kaye in the title roles. Meanwhile, the script has been put together by T.J Fixman, a *Ratchet & Clank* veteran who has written six games in the franchise. However, Sony have roped in some Hollywood names to bring some extra credibility to their project, something which may well come in handy given the terrible reputation video game movies have right now. Paul Giamatti, Sylvester Stallone, John Goodman and Rosario Dawson have joined the project in new roles, while taking on directing duties is Kevin Munroe who helmed the 2007 TMNT movie, who'll be co-directing with newcomer Jericca Cleland. Munroe doesn't have a very impressive list of films to his name, but has evidently pleased Sony given that they've also put him in charge of another of their animated videogame adaptations *Sly Cooper*. *Ratchet & Clank* is among three other films (*Angry Birds*, *Warcraft*, and *Assassin's Creed*) vying for the title of the first critically acclaimed videogame movie; we'll have to wait until April 29th to see if it can take the title.

Same Kind of Different as Me

After being dormant for about five years, Renée Zellweger's career has finally picked up again following her apparent plastic surgery-fuelled transformation which made headlines in 2014. In April, Zellweger stars in *Same Kind of Different as Me*, a faith-based drama based on a true story which follows Deborah – a religious woman who received a message from God telling her to save a man called Denver (played here by *Guardians of the Galaxy* star Djimon Hounsou). Deborah was later diagnosed with cancer, and Denver helped her carry on the ministry she had started as her health deteriorated. Based on the book of the same name, the film is to be directed by Michael Carney who'll be making his feature length directorial debut. Carney has also adapted the script alongside the book's original authors. If this film can strike a chord with audiences, it could be the start of a long-awaited comeback for Zellweger who will also soon be returning to the role for which she is best known: Bridget Jones.

May

6th May

Captain America: Civil War

Who would have thought that in 2011 when *Captain America: The First Avenger* came out to a relatively lukewarm response, that this franchise would go on to become one of the biggest guns in Marvel Studios' arsenal? Indeed, when it was announced that the studio was moving ahead with a second Captain America film, some felt that it was just a way for them to save face as the film had been the second weakest box office performer of Marvel's 'Phase One' line-up. The only film that performed weaker than *The First Avenger* was *The Incredible Hulk* which by that point had already been somewhat disowned thanks to star Edward Norton's apparently difficult behaviour during production. However, upon the release of *Captain America: The Winter Soldier,* Marvel Studios accomplished the seemingly impossible task of boosting Captain America's popularity up to levels that rivalled that of the jewel in their crown, Iron Man. It is then with high expectations that fans await the release of the third film in the franchise, *Civil War.*

Loosely based on the comic-book storyline of the same name, Civil War is essentially Avengers 2.5 with almost every member of the MCU scheduled to make an appearance, a prospect which has Marvel comic-book fans (myself among them) awaiting the film with delirious anticipation. For those unfamiliar, the comic-book story begins with a group of inexperienced young super-heroes provoking a villain into committing a horrifyingly destructive act, which results in the deaths of numerous young schoolchildren. The government response to this is the Superhuman Registration Act which demands all the heroes of the Marvel Universe give up their identities, so that they can be properly monitored and deployed only when the government sees fit. This leads to the Avengers breaking into two groups, with Tony Stark leading the pro-registration heroes, while Captain America goes underground with those heroes wanting to fight the new law.

Marvel Studios had something of a disappointing year in 2015. While it's true that *Avengers: Age of Ultron* made over a billion dollars, it's also true that the high-profile sequel failed to match the haul of the first instalment. Meanwhile, the studio's other release – *Ant-Man* – was a solid performer but didn't come anywhere close to the success that *Guardians of the Galaxy* experienced one year prior. So, it seems that *Civil War* really needs to be a hit in order to reassert Marvel Studios' dominance over the comic-book movie genre. The aforementioned expansive ensemble cast should help in filling up those all-important movie theatre seats, while the fact that the entire creative team from Cap's impressive second film have stuck around makes me optimistic that we could have another quality film on our hands.

Indeed, I've warned against piling enormous amounts of hype onto films multiple times already in this book, but with Captain America: Civil War I may prove myself to be a hypocrite and do exactly that. I am a self-confessed super-fan of the Marvel Cinematic Universe, and although I'm trying to be as level-headed as possible for the sake of this book, I'm finding it difficult to imagine that this film will be anything other than great. Isn't this bias, I hear you cry? Are these the ramblings of a Marvel 'fanboy' who took time to deconstruct the hype for *Batman v Superman*, but when discussing the latest Marvel feature can muster not a single negative word?

Absolutely not. While in all honesty I have enjoyed the recent Marvel Studios films more so than I have the last few DC offerings, I don't consider myself as allegiant to either side. In fact, I'm a firm believer that the ongoing Marvel vs. DC debate is utterly pointless; why unnecessarily choose one side when alternatively you can enjoy the fruits of both? My concerns about *Batman v Superman* come only as a DC fan who wants the best representation of these two iconic characters as possible, but feels that the current creative team may not be the best people to accomplish that goal. My overall lack of concern for *Civil War* on the other hand is a result of Marvel Studios relatively strong track record as of late, leaving me comfortable putting my faith in them. One day, it is my hope that the folks at Warner Bros. (the studio in charge of the DC properties) will acquire the same faith, but at the moment I simply have little reason to believe they could create something outstanding without the guiding hand of Christopher Nolan on-board.

Of course it is not out of the realm of possibility that *Civil War* could be terrible. Juggling such a large cast could lead to some overcrowding issues, and due to the nature of the Marvel Cinematic Universe (no secret identities, far fewer heroes than the comics etc.), the film adaptation of *Civil War* is going to have to take some liberties with the source material that may well end up being rejected by fans. But for the time being, if there's one film in this book that I think stands a chance at being my favourite of 2016, it is *Civil War*.

6th May
Going in Style

Opening opposite the juggernaut *Captain America: Civil War* we have *Going in Style*, a comedy heist film which appears to be targeting a different demographic altogether. Enlisting the A-List veteran actors Michael Caine, Morgan Freeman and Alan Arkin this film is a remake of the 1979 feature of the same name in which three retirees plan to rob a bank together. Older audiences are not to be underestimated when it comes to their box office prowess, and so the placement of this movie opposite the latest Marvel Studios flick could make it effective counter-programming for an audience which may not be enthused by super-hero blockbusters. *Going in Style* is being directed by *Scrubs* star Zach Braff, who impressed with his directorial debut *Garden State* before disappointing with his crowd-funded second feature *Wish I Was Here*. Perhaps working with such accomplished actors on this project will help bring out the best in Braff, who'll be directing a script written by Theodore Melfi who made his name writing the screenplay for another film with a lively retiree in the lead role – *St. Vincent* starring Bill Murray. Both *St. Vincent* and 2013's *Last Vegas* proved there's certainly an audience for films starring older leads, but whether *Going in Style* will find said audience in such a crowded summer remains to be seen.

20ᵗʰ May
Neighbours 2: Sorority Rising

When *Neighbours* (also known as *Bad Neighbours* to those outside of North America) was released in 2014, many heralded it as a breakout performance for Zac Efron. Efron of course made his name with the Disney Channel's *High School Musical* films, and since that franchise wrapped up has been trying to forge a successful film career in Hollywood. For a while it was uncertain just when that career would kick into high gear, with the romantic dramas he was seemingly confined to at first never really hitting big. In 2014 though, Efron tried reaching out to a new audience with the R-Rated comedies *That Awkward Moment* and the aforementioned *Neighbours*, the latter becoming the actor's highest grossing film to date. Indeed, after the success of *Neighbours* many in the film industry speculated that Efron could now acquire a much higher status in Hollywood; that was until 2015 brought Efron's aspirations crashing back down to Earth. Efron's solo vehicle following the buzz he garnered with *Neighbours* was the drama *We Are Your Friends*, about a struggling DJ who is taken under the wing of someone more established, only to end up falling in love with his mentor's girlfriend which needless to say turns things ugly. While box office expectations weren't high for the low-budget feature, it's safe to say that no one could have predicted just how low it would open. The film made $1.7 million in its opening weekend, the lowest debut of all time for a studio film released in more than 2,000 theatres. While it would be unfair to suggest that this opening was entirely Efron's fault – a mixed critical reception may also have turned people away from the film, as well as the inclusion of Emily Ratajkowski who many still hold a grudge against for her appearance in Robin Thicke's Blurred Lines music video – there's no denying that *We Are Your Friends* halted the new-found momentum that Efron's career had so recently received.

Down but not out, in 2016 Efron is returning to the genre that seems to hold the most promise for him as he stars in three R-rated comedies this year, the most notable being a sequel to his 2014 hit. While many comedy sequels have seen diminishing returns – both financially and creatively – *Neighbours 2* shows some promise. The first film was by no means outstanding, but it was an enjoyable feature with some very memorable characters. It is quite fortunate then that most cast members from the first film are returning including Seth Rogen, Rose Byrne, Dave Franco, Ike Barinholtz and of course Zac Efron, while Chloe Grace Moretz and Selena Gomez are also joining the sequel in new roles. Additionally, the behind-the-camera talent has also been carried forward, with the first film's screenwriting team also working on the sequel alongside returning director

Nicholas Stoller. It's comforting to see the first film's creative team retained, and exciting to see such strong additions to the cast – particularly Moretz who has proven herself to be a fantastic young actress but hasn't been involved in very many notable projects as of late. The plot will seemingly give Moretz one of her first antagonistic roles, as young couple Mac and Kelly (played by Rogen and Byrne) struggle after a group of sorority sisters move into their neighbouring house. Gomez and Moretz will presumably be playing the two leading sisters, giving them both a chance to stretch their comedic muscles. Ultimately, with a strong cast and crew I think the biggest challenge *Neighbours 2* will face is the same challenge faced by almost every comedy sequel: how not to exhaust the premise. The fact that this film is once again centred on a bunch of rowdy college kids moving in next door to a friendly young couple, makes me worry that *Neighbours 2* could feel very samey and hit many of the same beats as the first film. Of course the fact that it's now a bunch of girls next door rather than a bunch of guys could allow for some fresh material, but whether this will be enough to make the film a hit with film critics remains to be seen. Regardless, Efron in particular will be hoping the film is at least a financial success as he could use a hit in order to shake off the bad press he took in the wake of *We Are Your Friends* being an utter flop. The film opens stateside on the 20th May.

20th May
The Angry Birds Movie

At first glance this movie looks like an utter waste of time. Video game movies have failed time and time again to capture audiences, so how on Earth is a mobile game with no plot whatsoever to be translated successfully to the big screen? With great difficulty, probably. As I write this the first trailer for the *Angry Birds Movie* has very recently been released and it was...quite average. While I commend the writers of this project for injecting a story where there was none, it remains heavily shrouded in doubt whether doing so was a particularly good idea. From the trailer, the *Angry Birds Movie* appears to take place on an island inhabited only by birds, some of whom are angry as the title would suggest. When the island is boarded by pigs, conflict will presumably occur as the premise of the mobile game is something of a never-ending war between the two animals. While the trailer lacked any truly laugh-out-loud moments there were glimmers of good jokes here and there, and so perhaps foolishly I'm choosing not to give up on this film just yet. Another big reason I have for keeping faith in this movie is the fantastic cast that have assembled for it, a cast which includes Jason Sudeikis taking the lead while *Frozen*'s Josh Gad, *This is the End*'s Danny McBride, *Bridesmaids*' Maya Rudolph, *Trainwreck*'s Bill Hader and *Game of Thrones*' Peter Dinklage fill the supporting roles. Meanwhile the script has been written by Jon Vitti, a screenwriter who made a name for himself writing a number of memorable episodes of *The Simpsons* between its first and sixteenth seasons. So in spite of my initial reservations, there is actually quite solid talent behind this movie. Could it be then that the *Angry Birds* could surprise us, and bring the first widely-liked video game movie of all-time into existence? Well that's far from a safe bet, but there's certainly potential here and *The Angry Birds Movie* may well not be the write-off that it initially seemed it would be.

20th May

The Nice Guys

The Nice Guys is the latest film from Shane Black who made his directorial debut back in 2005 with the black comedy *Kiss Kiss Bang Bang*, before raising his profile in Hollywood significantly when he took on the job of directing *Iron Man 3* – which went on to become one of the highest-grossing films of all-time. In 2016, Black returns to screens with *The Nice Guys* a drama-thriller starring Ryan Gosling and Russell Crowe as two LA detectives, working together to solve the case of a missing girl and the seemingly unrelated death of an "adult film" actress. The film has generated a significant amount of buzz worldwide, with international distribution rights being snapped up remarkably quickly. However, the question remains whether that early buzz can be turned into ticket sales, especially as Gosling particularly has struggled to draw crowds with recent features *Gangster Squad* and *Only God Forgives*. Indeed, opening alongside *Angry Birds* and *Neighbours 2* with *X-Men Apocalypse* hitting screens just one week later, *The Nice Guys* will have no shortage of competition and will have to work hard to ensure it isn't lost in the chaos of the summer movie season.

27th May
X-Men: Apocalypse

Not long ago the *X-Men* film franchise was in a pretty unhealthy state indeed. While the films have always been dependable from a financial aspect, the successive critical disappointments of *X-Men: The Last Stand* and *X-Men Origins: Wolverine* risked alienating fans away from this long-running franchise. The decision then was made to take a grand departure from the first four instalments in the series, going all the way back to the 1960s to focus primarily on a young Professor X and Magneto. What followed was a remarkable turnaround in the critical fortunes of the franchise, with many saying that 2014's instalment *Days of Future Past* is the best in the series to date – a particularly impressive feat considering the negative publicity the film faced prior to release regarding the depiction of Quicksilver, and the changes made to the comic-book story on which the film was based.

With *X-Men: Apocalypse* the ball seems to be in the court of 20th Century Fox, who seem genuinely intent on continuing the repair of their franchise and taking it from strength to strength. Bryan Singer has returned to the director's chair for this instalment, with the writers of the generally well received X2 in tow. Not only are things looking promising behind the camera, but on-screen things are also shaping up well. James McAvoy,

Michael Fassbender and Jennifer Lawrence are reprising their roles from previous films, while *Apocalypse* is also giving Fox the chance to recast certain characters that comic-book fans feel weren't accurately portrayed the first time round.

These characters include Cyclops, Storm, Nightcrawler and Jean Grey who are recast with a far younger group of actors than we saw in the original *X-Men* trilogy. Indeed, I'm going to be totally honest and say my familiarity with these youngsters is minimal, partly because I haven't had the chance to catch up with their previous work, and partly because some of them really don't have that much work to catch up with. Alexandra Shipp (the new Storm) has the smallest body of work out of the new cast members, although it's worth noting that Sophie Turner (the new Jean Grey) also has a relatively small résumé outside of her role as Sansa Stark on HBO's *Game of Thrones*. Kodi Smit-McPhee (brought in to replace Alan Cumming's Nightcrawler) can be seen in 2014's excellent *Dawn of the Planet of the Apes*, while Tye Sheridan (the new Scott Summers aka Cyclops) cut his teeth on the indie circuit with the two somewhat similar films *Mud* and *Joe*. Of course, the decision to cast such young actors was no doubt done consciously by Fox; casting an actor in their youth means a franchise can get plenty of mileage out of them before they outgrow their role, while casting relative unknowns usually means a multiple-film contract can be signed on the cheap.

Thanks to some photos released from the set onto director Bryan Singer's Twitter account, fans have already caught their first glimpses of the new actors in their roles, and so far things are looking pretty good. A big complaint comic-book fans have had about the *X-Men* films in the past is the costume design; in the comics, the mutant super-team is home to some of the brightest and most extravagant costumes in the entire Marvel Universe, while in the films the *X-Men* have worn primarily black leather. Now to be fair to Fox, the first *X-Men* film came out when comic-book movies were far from the hot commodity they are today, and as a result bright and colourful costumes were swapped out for *Matrix*-esque costumes with the intention of not alienating mainstream audiences. Now though, what with the Marvel Cinematic Universe translating super-hero costumes to the big screen relatively faithfully, people are finally ready to see Wolverine in the yellow spandex outfit that James Marsden's Cyclops referenced back in 2000.

It is then comforting that, while still something of a leap from the comic-book incarnations, Fox do seem to be getting more adventurous with their costume choices in *X-Men: Apocalypse*. Our first look at Shipp confirmed that Storm would be sporting the much-beloved Mohawk that she fashioned in the comics in the early 1980s, a look that she recently revived in the Marvel comics currently being published. Meanwhile, Smit-McPhee's Nightcrawler costume has hints of the bright red that he's known for, and new additions to the team Psylocke and Jubilee (played by Olivia Munn and

Lana Condor respectively) look to be some of the most faithful costume designs the film series has ever seen.

However, Fox do have their limits; while the studio seem to have done their best with the new mutants, they may have let the side down when it comes to the big bad himself, Apocalypse. In the comics, Apocalypse is an ancient and hugely powerful mutant whose abilities allow him to channel almost any physical super-power. On top of this, the character is physically very large and intimidating; at his smallest, Apocalypse is about seven foot tall, but has been known to grow substantially taller. With all this taken into account, it's understandable that fans gave a mixed response to Singer and co.'s interpretation of the character which they claimed was reminiscent of the *Power Rangers* villain Ivan Ooze, which needless to say is not a compliment.

Still, as fun as it is for comic-book fans to pick apart the first images of their favourite characters making a foray into live-action, it's important not to write off these characters until we actually see them up on-screen. I recall the aforementioned bad press surrounding Evan Peters' Quicksilver in the run-up to the release of *X-Men: Days of Future Past*. Fans were almost universally convinced that the character would be poorly interpreted, as so many other mutants have been over the course of this franchise. Lo and behold, Quicksilver's brief appearance in *Days of Future Past* would end up being the best part of the film for many fans.

I guess what I'm saying is not to underestimate *X-Men: Apocalypse*. While 20th Century Fox have proven themselves capable of mishandling their Marvel properties in the past (see 2003's *Daredevil*) and indeed again very recently (see 2015's *Fantastic Four* reboot), their last two X-Men films have been very enjoyable features and there's no reason that *Apocalypse* can't follow suit. Fans of the marvel mutants are in for a bumper year in 2016, with *Apocalypse* sandwiched between two *X-Men* spin-offs, Ryan Reynold's *Deadpool* and Channing Tatum's *Gambit*.

27th May
Alice Through the Looking Glass

Given how mixed the critical reception was at the time of its release and just how much has come in the six years since then, I find that it's sometimes easy to forget just how successful Tim Burton's *Alice in Wonderland* film really was. The film made over one billion dollars and remains one of Disney's highest grossing projects of all time. It was inevitable then that we would be given the chance to return to Burton's surreal and CGI-heavy interpretation of Lewis Carroll's classic fantasy story; what is more surprising though is that Burton is no longer at the helm. Indeed, the prolific director has chosen to return only as a producer for this second outing, with James Bobin replacing him in the director's chair. Bobin is in good-standing with Disney having made two feature films for them in recent years: *The Muppets* and *Muppets Most Wanted*. While neither were huge box office performers, you can assume that both pleased the higher-ups at Disney given that they chose to hire him for this far more high-profile project. *Alice Through The Looking Glass* sees the return of Mia Wasikowska to the role of Alice Kingsleigh, alongside other returning stars Johnny Depp as the Mad Hatter, Helena Bonham Carter as the Red Queen and Anne Hathaway as the White Queen among many others.

Buzz for this movie has been generally quite muted as a result of the aforementioned mixed reception that the first film received, and so perhaps the most interesting thing about *Alice Through the Looking Glass* will be whether it can perform anywhere near as well as the first film – especially considering it's opening against the much-anticipated *X-Men: Apocalypse*. One of the major selling points of *Alice in Wonderland* was its use of 3D technology, however six years later this technology is not only less interesting to movie-goers but some would say it has worn out its welcome entirely. Meanwhile, in the time since 2010 we've seen the rapid degradation of Johnny Depp's career who has added a number of flops to his résumé including *Dark Shadows*, *Transcendence*, *Mortdecai* and most notably *The Lone Ranger*. When you factor in the bad taste that audiences may still have left in their mouths from the first film, it paints a picture which depicts *Alice Through the Looking Glass* as a sure-fire flop. However, there is hope yet that the film could avoid such a fate. The addition of a new director could make the film just fresh enough to convince movie-goers to give this series another chance. Another thing to consider is that while some would see opening against *X-Men: Apocalypse* as a bad sign for Alice and co., it's worth remembering that two of 2015's biggest hits weren't comic-book movies: *Jurassic World* and *Furious 7*. This seems to suggest that many people are perhaps looking to take a break from the world of caped super-heroes – and *Alice Through the Looking Glass* could provide just the relief they're looking for.

30th May
USS Indianapolis: Men of Courage

Nicholas Cage is an actor who sadly has lost a lot of his credibility in recent years, mainly due to his tendency to say yes to pretty much every script that's put in front of him. As a result, it's hard to get excited for Cage's upcoming movie *USS Indianapolis: Men of Courage*, especially after a particularly bad couple of years which have seen the critically panned dramas *Dying of the Light* and *Left Behind* unleashed on audiences. *Men of Courage* is set during World War II and tells the true story of a crew whose ship was torpedoed in the South Pacific after delivering parts for the first atomic bombs. This film does appear to be one of the more reputable productions Cage has taken part in recently, with the construction of a 500,000 gallon water tank showing some dedication to telling this story as well as possible. Still, whether this movie will be of any quality whatsoever is still unclear especially with unproven director Mario Van Peebles at the helm whose previous directing gigs consist primarily of episodes of TV shows such as *Once Upon a Time*, *Nashville*, and *Empire*. Ultimately, I'd approach this film with great caution; it's unfortunate but the fact remains that at this point if Nicholas Cage has the lead role in a film, then that's less of a selling point and more of an alarm bell. As a result, it might be an idea to check out what the critics have to say before rushing out to see *Men of Courage*.

June

3rd June
Teenage Mutant Ninja Turtles: Half Shell

2014's *Teenage Mutant Ninja Turtles* may have been critically reviled, but there's no denying that the film from producer Michael Bay made these iconic characters relevant once more. Indeed, after 2007's financial disappointment *TMNT* it was unclear whether the heroes in a half shell would ever be the face of a successful film franchise again. However, after Bay applied a similar tactic to that which he gave the ever-popular *Transformers* movies – mainly CGI-heavy action sequences and some objectification of women – the turtles were once again a powerful force in Hollywood with their comeback flick bringing in just shy of $500 million. Whether this sequel can bring in the same number after the critical mauling received by its first instalment remains to be seen, but given that the *Transformers* franchise has somehow powered through critical hatred to grow more profitable with each entry

I'd say it isn't such a long shot that this franchise could go from strength to strength.

Hey, there's even a chance this sequel could be far better than the first – it's admittedly wishful thinking, but it isn't out of the realm of possibility. For *Half Shell*, Paramount Pictures has brought in a new director in the form of Dave Green who made his directorial debut in 2013 with the family sci-fi feature *Earth to Echo*. Now, while *Earth to Echo* was by no means beloved it did receive a far warmer reception than 2014's *Turtles* movie, and most critics were agreed it was a fine distraction for young children in spite of being somewhat derivative of Steven Spielberg's 1982 classic *E.T.* Additionally, something that seems to have pleased fans of the Ninja Turtles was the casting of Stephen Amell as vigilante Casey Jones. Jones was created in 1985 as a parody of vigilante characters, and so seeing Amell take on the role – an actor who has made his name playing such a character on the TV series *Arrow* – is something which has gone down well with fans alienated by the 2014 movie.

Still though, while these developments are promising it is worth noting that *Half Shell* sees the writers and producers – Michael Bay among them – carried over from the first film, and so it does seem unlikely that this sequel will be much different than the critically-maligned debut of the revamped turtles. The second instalment also sees the cast of the first return, with Alan Ritchson, Noel Fisher, Johnny Knoxville and Jeremy Howard reprising their roles as the motion-capture Ninja Turtles, while Megan Fox and Will Arnett return as characters April O'Neill and Vern Fenwick.

Ultimately, I think this is another case of if you liked the first film then there may be something for you here, but if like many people you found yourself disappointed the first time round it's unlikely that anything will have changed two years later.

3rd June
Conner4real

Conner4real is the second film from comedy music group *The Lonely Island*, the first being 2007's *Hot Rod* which performed relatively badly upon initial release but has since gained a cult following. *Conner4real* is the story of a rapper (played by perhaps the most well-known member of *The Lonely Island*, Andy Samberg), who is forced to reunite his old boy band after his rap album bombs. With this premise it appears the film will be playing up the group's musical talents, as the other members of *The Lonely Island* Akiva Schaffer and Jorma Taccone take the two other lead roles. Schaffer and Taccone are also directing the film together, while the cast also features comedian Sarah Silverman, *The Inbetweeners*' James Buckley, *28 Weeks Later*'s Imogen Poots and *Mean Girls*' Tim Meadows. While *The Lonely Island*'s first production did receive a mixed response, *Conner4real* stands a chance of correcting the areas where *Hot Rod* went wrong. The comedy group's popularity has skyrocketed since 2007, thanks to the release of three albums and the increased fanbase of

Andy Samberg following his casting in the hit FOX sitcom *Brooklyn Nine-Nine*. With the increased exposure they've been receiving along with the nine years they've had to hone their craft, there's a good chance *Conner4real* could go above and beyond expectations and make *The Lonely Island*'s fan following even greater.

3rd June
Me Before You

Me Before You is a romantic drama based on the novel of the same name which follows Lou Clark, a woman whose life is plunged into chaos after she loses her job at a local tea shop. She eventually crosses paths with Will Traynor, a man who became deeply depressed after a motorcycle accident left him unable to use his legs. The relationship that follows changes both lives forever. The response to the novel has been largely positive, however it's questionable just how well it will translate to the big screen. It is after all, coming from a director relatively new to the film industry Thea Sharrock, who has earned most of her directing credits working on theatre productions. Still, there is a chance Sharrock will be able to successfully transition from theatre to film, and she does have a solid cast here to help her achieve that goal. *Game of Thrones*' Emilia Clarke takes the lead no doubt hoping this film will do some damage control after her 2015 embarrassment *Terminator Genisys*. Meanwhile, *The Hunger Games*' Sam Claflin and veteran actor Charles Dance also star alongside *Doctor Who* companion Jenna Coleman, who may be looking to launch a film career after recently leaving the long-running science-fiction program. Good romance can be hard to convey effectively and countless films have fallen into overly-sentimental territory, but given that this film has kept the author of *Me Before You* Jojo Moyes on board to help with the screenplay perhaps this adaptation will avoid the pitfalls others in this genre have fallen into. The film will be released on the 3rd June.

10th June

Warcraft

Hollywood has been making films out of videogames for quite some time now, with the first attempt being in 1993 with the infamous and critically mauled *Super Mario Bros.* movie starring Bob Hoskins. Since then, twenty seven other videogame adaptations have seen release and not a single one has been widely well received – in fact, some of them (particularly those helmed by the loathed director Uwe Boll) have secured places on more than a few 'Worst Films of All-Time' lists. That hasn't stopped some from being financial successes, with Angelina Jolie's brief run as Lara Croft bringing in some solid returns, Aaron Paul's 2014 *Need for Speed* film also turning a decent profit, while Milla Jovovich's *Resident Evil* films seem to be the most enduring of the bunch with five instalments already released and a sixth on its way in 2017.

But why are these movies consistently panned by critics, especially when the games that spawned them are usually critically acclaimed? It's hard to say for sure, but some have theorised that translating the highly interactive medium of videogames to the somewhat detached medium of film is a deceivingly difficult task. Others say that those in charge of making these films are out of touch with the source material, and rather than attempt to understand why the fandom around the games they're adapting is so strong, are instead too focused on tapping in to the potentially lucrative profits that their pie charts and graphs tell them is ripe for the taking. Some have even said that film studios should stop trying to adapt videogames into film altogether, that the two mediums are simply too different to merge successfully and should simply be left alone. But – as I've already mentioned in reference to April's *The Huntsman* – Hollywood will never let a potential cash-cow rest until they've milked it for all it's got, and so 2016 has consequentially become the biggest year videogame movies have ever seen with four adaptations set to hit theatres. By the time *Warcraft* is released in June, two of those adaptations will have already come and gone – the computer animated family-friendly features, *Ratchet and Clank* and *The Angry Birds Movie*.

As the first live-action videogame movie of the year, as well as the long-awaited adaptation of one of the biggest games on the planet, all eyes will be on *Warcraft* when it releases June 3rd. *World of Warcraft* developers Blizzard Entertainment have been working on getting their franchise to the screen since 2006, with Sam Raimi attached to the project for a time while the aforementioned Uwe Boll also tried to get his hands on the project at one point too. Fortunately for us all, that never happened. After numerous delays and script rewrites, the wheels really started turning in January 2013 when Duncan Jones – director of the critically acclaimed films *Moon* and *Source Code* – was announced to be taking on directing duties. Since then hype has slowly been building around this project, with Jones giving himself some lofty expectations to live up to through comparing his *Warcraft* movie to the juggernaut franchises *Game of Thrones* and *Avatar*. It has been announced that the film will follow both sides of a conflict between the humans and the orcs, supposedly not outright portraying either side as the 'bad guys'.

Surprisingly for a film with a budget reportedly over $100 million, *Warcraft* doesn't star any actors that could reasonably be considered as "big names." The human side of the conflict will feature Travis Fimmel of the History Channel's *Vikings*, Dominic Cooper who is known to Marvel fans as young Howard Stark, and Ben Foster whose most notable work would be supporting roles in forgettable action films such as *Contraband* and *The Mechanic*. On the side of the orcs we have Toby Kebbell, last seen in the critically panned 2015 *Fantastic Four* reboot, with *Pacific Rim*'s Rob Kazinsky also to feature prominently. However, the orc characters are likely to be dressed up in prosthetics or hidden behind CGI characters and so what little star power these two actors had may well end up being lost. Jones has said that the film will feature female characters with important parts to play, with *Agents of S.H.I.E.L.D*'s Ruth Negga and

Mission: Impossible's Paula Patton presumably filling these roles.

Ultimately it seems that Legendary Pictures is relying on the very famous videogame brand to get people into cinemas, rather than roping in an all-star cast to do that job instead. A risky strategy, but one that might just work – especially if *Warcraft* receives the same warm critical reception as Duncan Jones' previous two films, an achievement which would make it the first ever critically-acclaimed live-action videogame adaptation. There does appear to have been more effort made to deliver a quality film than we have seen put into any videogame adaptation before it. The concept of not having an antagonist, but merely two opposing sides each with their own protagonist is a genuinely interesting idea that we haven't seen much in recent Hollywood blockbusters, and the rising interest in fantasy at the moment thanks to projects like *Game of Thrones* and *The Hobbit* means that the atmosphere may be just right for *Warcraft* to be a big hit with mainstream movie-goers. Overall, I'm cautiously optimistic about this project, but given Hollywood's frankly quite dreadful track record when it comes to movies based on videogames, I may be a fool for getting my hopes up.

10th June

The Conjuring 2: The Enfield Poltergeist

Director James Wan burst onto the horror scene back in 2003 with a gruesome short film that was just under ten minutes long, that short film was called *Saw*. The disturbing project – which followed a man who had been drugged, and awoke with his head locked in a so-called 'reverse bear trap' – was screened for film studio Lionsgate who immediately agreed to expand it into a feature-length film. The rest, as they say, is history. The *Saw* franchise quickly became one of the biggest horror film series' of all-time, spawning six sequels which Wan produced but chose not to direct so to avoid being known as 'the *Saw* guy'. Indeed, the director's search for new projects to helm began unsuccessfully, and led to him directing two critical and commercial flops in 2007: the similarly titled *Dead Silence* and *Death Sentence*. But eventually Wan struck gold once again with 2010's *Insidious*, a film that seemed to kick his career back into high gear. Since *Insidious* Wan's career has gone from strength to strength, with the man's hard work seemingly coming to a head in 2015 when his first foray into action filmmaking – *Furious 7* – grossed over $1.5 billion, making it one of the highest-grossing films of all time.

In 2016, Wan returns to the genre in which he made his name, with a sequel to his most acclaimed film: *The Conjuring*. Following the supposedly true events experienced by paranormal investigators Ed and Lorraine Warren, the first *Conjuring* movie was released to a warm reception from critics and so it is with high expectations that fans await the second film. Stars Patrick Wilson and Vera Farmiga are returning for the sequel, which will see another of the Warren's most famous cases adapted for the screen. The Enfield Poltergeist was a case involving two young girls aged eleven and thirteen, who were seemingly affected by poltergeist activity in the years 1977 to 1979. Whether or not you believe these stories to be true – something which is still the cause of some debate to this day – with Wan at the helm there's a good chance that these events will at least be translated to an effective horror feature. Indeed, while Wan has certainly had slip-ups during his journey to the top, all of his films post-*Insidious* have been entertaining offerings, and this has given him a degree of credibility among most film fans. *The Conjuring 2* is also significant for being only something of a pit-stop for Wan, who will be taking yet another break from the horror circuit in the years following this film's release, this time to work on Warner Bros. upcoming *Aquaman* movie starring Jason Momoa which Wan is directing. Fans of the genre may not be too pleased to hear of Wan's second departure; especially as mainstream Hollywood studios continue to show a misunderstanding over how to pull off a compelling horror story, a fact evident in the critically panned *Conjuring* spin-off *Annabelle* which Wan had relatively little involvement in.

The fact that Warner Bros. have chosen to give *The Conjuring 2* a summer release date sandwiched between two high profile projects – *Warcraft* and *Finding Dory* – suggests that they have great faith that the film will be able to find an audience in spite of the fierce competition. We'll see if that faith pays off at the box office, when the film is released on the 10th June.

Now You See Me: The Second Act

When *Now You See Me* saw release in the summer of 2013, relatively little was expected of the movie given that it didn't star any talent that Hollywood considered being 'big names'. However, against the odds the movie following a group of illusionists became one of the surprise hits of that year, something that perhaps was helped by the fact that the film opened on the same weekend as *After Earth*. Indeed, the Will Smith sci-fi action film garnered so much bad publicity before release it was practically dead on arrival, and left many movie-goers flocking to the second biggest release of the week: *Now You See Me*. After a run which ended with a total gross of $350 million it wasn't surprising to see a sequel greenlit. *The Second Act* sees much of the main cast returning including Mark Ruffalo, Woody Harrelson and perhaps most notably Jesse Eisenberg, who should be on a career-high if *Batman v Superman* is the hit everyone is expecting it to be. Meanwhile, the film has added some new faces in the form of *Mean Girls*' Lizzy Caplan and the boy wizard himself Daniel Radcliffe. The former was brought in to replace Isla Fisher who couldn't return due to her pregnancy, while the latter is taking the film's antagonistic role – something which could be an interesting change of pace for the actor who is typically cast as a protagonist, no doubt as a result of his years as the face of the *Harry Potter* franchise. It's hard to delve into whom specifically Radcliffe will be playing without spoiling the plot of the first film, but to put it vaguely he's a character with a grudge against the gang of magicians made up by the main cast.

The writer of the first film Ed Solomon returns for the sequel, while the director Louis Leterrier has been swapped out for Jon M. Chu. Chu is something of an odd choice for *The Second Act* given that most of his previous films have had a rather hostile reaction from critics, with most being of the dance/music genre e.g. *Step Up 2*, *Step Up 3D*, the Justin Bieber concert films and *Jem and the Holograms*. Regardless of this unimpressive résumé Lionsgate have put him in charge of the sequel, and must have a lot of faith in him given that they're currently looking to expand this franchise even further, with a third *Now You See Me* film currently in the works. How big *The Second Act* opens really depends on how many long-lasting fans the first film created, along with what the critical reception of *Warcraft* ends up being. If it is indeed the first well-received live-action videogame movie then *The Second Act* could have an uphill struggle on its hands here, but if it garners the same bad reviews that both *After Earth* and almost every previous videogame movie suffered from then this franchise could triumph in the ashes of a DOA blockbuster once again.

17th June
Finding Dory

It's no secret that, outside of the *Toy Story* films, Pixar Animation hasn't had a lot of luck with its sequels – at least in terms of critical reception.

Indeed, Cars 2 is widely recognised as the worst film the studio has ever made, while *Monsters University* was a solid but unremarkable feature which lacked much of the originality of the first instalment. This unimpressive track record combined with the fact that Pixar recently went into something of a creative slump – which actually led to the studio choosing not to release a film in 2014 in order to reassess their current situation – has led to fears over the quality of the upcoming *Finding Dory*. While their 'year out' strategy seems to have had a positive effect so far, with 2015's *Inside Out* being seen as a triumphant return to form for the studio, this doesn't change the fact that Pixar are yet to produce a widely loved **sequel** that doesn't feature Woody, Buzz and the rest of Andy's toys.

Set about six months after 2003's *Finding Nemo*, this film sees Ellen DeGeneres' Dory take centre stage as she journeys across the ocean with the hope of being reunited with her family. The most worrying thing about this project for me is the fact that *Finding Nemo* really doesn't seem like a film crying out for a sequel. The instant-classic from 2003 tells a very intimate story about a family finally coming together after years of struggle, and by its end that story feels rather complete. A sequel involving yet another member of the family getting lost feels forced at first glance, coming off as (dare I say it) a cash-grab.

Still, let's not give up all hope just yet. *Finding Dory* sees the writer/director of the first film Andrew Stanton return to both duties once again; Stanton is a Pixar veteran having not just worked on *Finding Nemo*, but also other gems such as *Wall-E* and *Toy Story 3*. While his short-lived move to live-action was wholly unsuccessful, seeing him direct one of the most expensive flops of all time with *John Carter*, Stanton has proven himself as very capable in the realm of animation. Meanwhile, cast members from the first film such as Albert Brooks (Marlin) and Willem Dafoe (Gill) are already confirmed to be returning, with Ellen DeGeneres reprising the title role with much enthusiasm. DeGeneres is a woman whose career seems to be going from strength to strength, with her famous Oscar-selfie catapulting her to new levels of fame back in 2014.

Finding Dory will also see some new characters joining the returning cast members in the form of Kaitlin Olson and Idris Elba. Olson has made a name for herself on the superb FX sitcom *It's Always Sunny in Philadelphia*, and judging from her comedic timing on that show she should give an excellent performance as Destiny, a shark who believes she is a whale. Elba seems to be everybody's favourite actor at the moment and so I'm sure his addition in an as-of-yet undisclosed role will draw some people in, although I have to say I think the man is a little over-rated so personally his involvement fails to raise my anticipation for the film.

2016 is the beginning of a new era for Pixar Animation, an era in which sequels will be commonplace. Indeed, coming down the pipeline after *Finding Dory* we have *Toy Story 4*, the long-awaited *Incredibles 2*, and the less-eagerly anticipated *Cars 3*. It is then of paramount importance that *Finding Dory* is well received by audiences, because if the studio can't prove that they can produce worthwhile sequels outside of the *Toy Story* franchise, then they risk dragging their reputation through the dirt with these upcoming projects.

17th June

Central Intelligence

Central Intelligence is a comedy starring Dwayne 'The Rock' Johnson and Kevin Hart following an effective but immature CIA agent (Johnson), who returns to his hometown for a school reunion where he enlists the help of a former high school sports star (Hart) for a classified mission. Both are on something of a hot streak at the moment, with Johnson recently bagging a role as DC super-villain Black Adam while scoring two box office wins in 2015 with *San Andreas* and *Furious 7*. Meanwhile Hart has also been catching people's attention, as the comedian-turned-actor has been the face of a number of successful features as of late including *Ride Along*, *The Wedding Ringer*, and *Get Hard*. Interestingly, not one of those films were well-received by critics, which suggests that Hart is at a point in his career where his star power is able to overcome bad word of mouth. But you need only look to the likes of Vince Vaughn and Adam Sandler to see that people's tolerance doesn't last forever, and so Hart should really be working to make *Central Intelligence* more of a crowd-pleaser than his previous offerings.

The film is being directed by Rawson Marshall Thurber, best known for his work on *Dodgeball: A True Underdog*

Story and 2013's *We're The Millers*. Both films had a solid critical reception and both also turned a sizeable profit, meaning there's a very capable comedy filmmaker at the helm here. Thurber has also had a hand in the script along with his *We're The Millers* writers Sean Anders and John Morris. I'm hesitant to say that this movie will be one to watch, mainly because Hart has proven over the last couple of years that he isn't great at picking good projects to star in. Still, I am hoping that this film delivers as 2015's *Spy* reminded us just how entertaining the action-comedy genre can be when done right.

24th June

Independence Day: Resurgence

And finally, June ends with a bang as the long awaited sequel to the 1996 blockbuster *Independence Day* hits theatres. The film takes place twenty years after the events of the first and follows the chaos that ensues when reinforcements of the alien race defeated in the first film, finally receive a distress signal informing them of the first wave's failure. Cue another invasion filled with more over-the-top action. First off, we should probably address the elephant in the room here, that being Will Smith's absence in this sequel. His decision not to return can be put down to two main factors; the first is that the actor had a genuinely busy schedule and the filming of *After Earth* and *Suicide Squad* got in the way of his *Independence Day* return. However, perhaps the more notable reason Smith didn't stick around was

20th Century Fox's refusal to cough up the hefty pay cheque that Smith demanded in return for his appearance in the sequel: $50 million. While such a pay day isn't unheard of in Hollywood – indeed Robert Downey Jr. was paid $50 million as a bonus on top of his initial pay cheque after the success of the first *Avengers* film – it proved to be too much of an ask considering Smith hasn't been at the top of his game as of late (see the financial disappointments *After Earth* and *Focus*). So Smith won't be returning, but just as the first film helped establish him as a movie star, perhaps the second will help catapult another actor to stardom: Jessie Usher. Usher has a relatively small résumé at the time of writing, but being cast as the stepson of Will Smith's character could kick his career into high gear if this sequel is as successful as its predecessor. Joining Usher are two other up and coming actors Maika Monroe and Liam Hemsworth, the former having gained buzz on the indie films *The Guest* and *It Follows* and the latter making his name in *The Hunger Games* series. The casting of this young talent seems to be an attempt to modernise this relatively old franchise, as those behind this film seem to be taking steps to make *Independence Day: Resurgence* a representation of modern society. The US President is to be played by a woman (*CSI: NY*'s Sela Ward) and an announcement which made headlines during this film's production was that an openly gay character would play a pivotal role.

Having said that, *Independence Day: Resurgence* isn't abandoning its past and some cast members from the first film will be reprising their roles including Jeff

Goldblum (who's rumoured to be the lead character), Bill Pullman and Brent Spiner. They'll once again be working with the director of the first film, the prolific Roland Emmerich whose work post-*Independence Day* has been released to a lukewarm reception from critics time and time again. A common complaint that has followed Emmerich to almost all of his subsequent projects including 1998's *Godzilla*, *The Day After Tomorrow*, *10,000 BC* and *2012* is that his films are usually visually impressive but are severely lacking in terms of plot. I fear this complaint could rear its head again with *Independence Day: Resurgence*, but that doesn't necessarily mean the film won't be a success. There's definitely an audience out there for ridiculous action films that don't require much brainpower, and I know that because I've been a member of said audience multiple times in the past. Perhaps as a result, I wouldn't say there's anything too terrible about that either – to me, films are kind of like food groups. Dumb action films are comparable to the fatty, unhealthy food group, i.e. it probably isn't a good idea to sustain yourself on only those kinds of films, but likewise you shouldn't be ashamed to allow yourself some meaningless fun from time to time. With this in mind, I'm awaiting *Independence Day 2* with some optimism as while it likely won't be too thought provoking it could provide the kind of explosive fun I haven't found at the cinema since 2013's *Pacific Rim*. The film is at the time of writing the only major release coming down the pipeline on the 24th June, and if successful then it could lead to a third

Independence Day film if rumours spreading across the Internet are to be believed.

That's A Wrap!

That's all for this volume of *The Complete Guide to 2016 Movies*, I really hope you enjoyed reading. The second volume which will cover films being released in the months of July to December 2016 is currently planned for release in the spring of the same year.

I would just like to take a moment to thank my family for putting up with me secluding myself for about two and a half months in order to get this thing finished. My thanks also go out to film writers and bloggers that have inspired me to learn more about this fantastic industry: Grace Randolph, Mark Kermode, comicbookgirl19 and the folks at Red Letter Media chief among them. Also a big thanks to CreateSpace for giving countless writers the opportunity to see their work published. Finally, thanks to Tim Berners-Lee for inventing the World Wide Web, I doubt I could have written this book without it.

About the Author

David Craig is a writer living in the United Kingdom. He created his blog, *The Entertainment Network* in the summer of 2011 and has been updating it ever since with news stories, reviews and features about the entertainment industry. In 2015, he founded another blog *TEN: Politics* which reports on global news stories. David has also written for other websites namely *What Culture* and *Comic Bastards*, and also makes YouTube videos. The videos do not get many views, leading him to the assumption that he must be an Internet superstar in a parallel universe. David's hobbies include writing about himself in the third person.

The Entertainment Network:

Website:
http://mediareviewsfeaturesandmore.blogspot.com
YouTube: www.youtube.com/EntertainmentNews123
Facebook:
www.facebook.com/entertainmentnewsandmore
Twitter: www.twitter.com/_thenetwork

TEN: Politics:

Website: http://tenpolitics.blogspot.co.uk
Facebook: www.facebook.com/tenpolitics
Twitter: www.twitter.com/tenpolitics